DATE DUE

KNOWING CHRISTIANITY

THE CHRISTIAN FAITH

KNOWING CHRISTIANITY

A series edited by Dr. William Neil to provide for thinking laymen a solid but non-technical presentation of what the Christian religion is and what it has to say in this atomic age.

The first titles are:

THE CHRISTIAN FAITH
THE OLD TESTAMENT

KNOWING CHRISTIANITY

The
Christian Faith

by

F. W. DILLISTONE
D.D.

J. B. LIPPINCOTT COMPANY

Philadelphia and New York

Printed in the United States of America. Library
of Congress Catalog Card Number: 64-23473

EDITOR'S PREFACE

To judge by the unending flow of religious literature from the various publishing houses there is an increasingly large demand on the part of ordinary intelligent people to know more about what Christianity has to say. This series is designed to help to meet this need and to cater for just this kind of people.

It assumes that there is a growing body of readers, both inside and outside the Church, who are prepared to give serious attention to the nature and claims of the Christian faith, and who expect to be given by theologians authoritative and up-to-date answers to the kind of questions thinking people want to ask.

More and more it becomes clear that we are unlikely to get any answers that will satisfy the deepest needs of the human spirit from any other quarter. Present-day science and philosophy give us little help on the ultimate questions of human destiny. Social, political and educational panaceas leave most of us unpersuaded. If we are not to end our quest for the truth about ourselves and the world we live in in cynicism and disillusionment where else can we turn but to religion?

Too often in the past two thousand years the worst advertisement for Christianity has been its supporters and advocates. Yet alone of all the great world religions it has shown that a faith which was oriental in origin could be transplanted into the western world and from there strike root again in the east. The present identification of Christianity in the minds of Asians and Africans with European culture and western capitalism or imperialism is a passing phase. To say that no other religion has the same potentialities as a world-wide faith for everyman is neither to denigrate the God-given truth in Buddhism, Islam and the rest, nor to say that at this stage Christianity as generally practised and understood in the west presents much more than a caricature of its purpose.

Perhaps the best corrective to hasty judgment is to measure these two thousand years against the untold millions of years of man's development. Organized Christianity is still in its infancy, as is the mind of man as he seeks to grapple with truths that could only come to him by revelation. The half has not yet been told and the full implications for human thought and action of the coming of God in Christ have as yet been only dimly grasped by most of us.

It is as a contribution to a deeper understanding of the mystery that surrounds us that this series is offered. The early volumes deal, as is only right, with fundamental issues —the historical impact of Christianity upon mankind based upon its Jewish origins and establishing itself in the wider world; the essence of the Christian faith and the character of Christian behaviour. Later volumes in the series will deal with various aspects of Christian thought and practice in relation to human life in all its variety and with its perennial problems.

The intention is to build up over the years a library which under the general title of 'Knowing Christianity' will provide for thinking laymen a solid but non-technical

6

presentation of what the Christian religion is and what it has to say in this atomic age.

The writers invited to contribute to this series are not only experts in their own fields but are all men who are deeply concerned that the gulf should be bridged between the specialized studies of the theologian and the untheologically minded average reader who nevertheless wants to know what theology has to say. I am sure that I speak in the name of all my colleagues in this venture when I express the hope that this series will do much to bridge the gap.

William Neil

The University,
Nottingham

AUTHOR'S PREFACE

THIS book seeks to interpret the Christian faith in a direct and personal way by asking how it is related to the basic structures of human life as we know them today. An alternative method of approach would have been through a backward look at history—to enquire how the Faith came to be expressed in the great Creeds and Confessions of the Church, to show how its formulation at any particular period was influenced by the cultural tendencies of the age. But I have attempted rather to look again at the Biblical witness to the nature and activity of God and to ask how this is related to our present situation.

I realize, of course, that it is impossible to jump over the centuries. The original witness was historically conditioned and it has been mediated to us through a long process of historical transmission. Yet there are certain patterns of human imagination and certain structures of human development which seem to be almost unaffected by the passage of time. These were available to receive the particular revelation of the glory of God to which the Bible bears its testimony. They are still available as symbolic forms or images through which the revelation can be expressed.

Taking four patterns of imagery which are common to human experience in Biblical times and in our contemporary world I have tried to express through them the threefold New Testament confession of faith in God. Or to put it in

9

another way I have tried to express the doctrine of the Trinity through the medium of four perennial symbolic forms. To some, I recognize, this may seem to be a dangerous narrowing down of the Christian faith. They may well ask whether sufficient attention has been given to the complex doctrines of the Incarnation and the Atonement, the Church and the Sacraments, Sanctification and Eternal Life, and I readily agree that a full-scale system of theology would need to treat these in considerable detail. Yet in presenting a personal interpretation of the Christian faith nothing, I believe, should be allowed to distract the attention from the central doctrine of the Trinity and its relation to the basic structures of human life.

I have found encouraging support for such a conviction in a quotation which has recently come to my notice. It occurs in an article contributed to the first number of *Studia Liturgica* by A. M. Allchin, the Librarian of Pusey House, Oxford. Seeking to define the doctrinal core of the Liturgical Movement he quotes a striking passage from a letter of a nineteenth century Anglican writer, R. M. Benson. "I am very glad," it reads "of what you say about the doctrine of the Blessed Trinity. It does seem to me to be the root evil of the present day, the want of pure theology. People are full of disputes about sacraments, eternal punishment, inspiration and the like; and yet the people who know a great deal about these controversies know next to nothing about the Holy Trinity. *But this is the Creed* (my italics). The others are only corollaries of the Creed and are helpful or hurtful just in proportion as they are made subservient to this fundamental doctrine—valueless, even when rightly held, if their connections with the eternal relationships of the Blessed

Trinity is not recognized. Our doctrine, teaching, experi-- ence of the Church, must be, so to speak, in a comatose state, unless there be an active, experimental, living know- ledge of the Name of the Holy Trinity, which is the living power wherewith the Church is bound together by the Holy Ghost.''

I believe with all my heart that the earliest Christian witnesses had an ''active, experimental, living knowledge of the Name of the Holy Trinity''. My aim has been to point the way to a re-discovery of that active, experimental, living knowledge within the context of our contemporary world.

CONTENTS

		Page
EDITOR'S PREFACE		5
AUTHOR'S PREFACE		9

Chapter

I	THE ESSENCE OF FAITH	15
II	THE HUMAN SITUATION	27
III	THE FAMILY OF GOD	40
IV	THE REDEEMED SOCIETY	68
V	THE HEAVENLY CITY	98
VI	DISCIPLES OF THE TRUTH	129
VII	I BELIEVE IN GOD	159

ABBREVIATIONS

A.V.	Authorized Version of the Bible 1611
R.S.V.	Revised Standard Version 1952
N.E.B.	New English Bible 1961

Chapter One

THE ESSENCE OF FAITH

Towards the end of the year 1961 the Editor of the periodical *Twentieth Century* selected a simple title for his Autumn issue: it was 'The Gods'. More than a dozen contributors examined the present state of religion in the world and discussed its future prospects. To Sir Julian Huxley was allotted the task of opening the debate by stating the case against God and the gods. This he did, first by dismissing Christianity as no longer relevant to our modern world and secondly by expounding his own conviction that some kind of evolutionary humanism must now take its place.

In reading Sir Julian's article, I found it particularly interesting to notice how he defines the essential beliefs of Christianity. He begins with the conception of a supernatural being, possessing properties akin to those of a human personality. This being is regarded as having created the world and man at a definite date in the past and as bringing the created order to judgment at a definite date in the future. He then refers to the belief in God's power to work miracles and to reveal Himself to man. In particular he dwells on the claim that the son of God was incarnate and rose from the dead for man's salvation. Concluding his brief survey he writes:

"This system of beliefs is quite unacceptable in the world of to-day. It is contradicted, as a whole and in detail, by our

extended knowledge of the cosmos, of the solar system, of our
own planet, of our own species and of our individual selves.''

Now it would obviously be impertinent to suggest that
Sir Julian is deficient in his knowledge of the cosmos and of
the structures of human life. But it is entirely in order to
raise questions about his knowledge of Christian doctrine.
Has he given a fair representation of essential Christian
beliefs? Has he ever listened sympathetically to an exposition of the creed by a trained Christian theologian? Has he
ever conversed at depth with a simple Christian believer?
Whether he has or not, it is quite certain that many who are
prepared to make pronouncements today about Christian
doctrine have little knowledge of the way in which this body
of doctrine has come into existence, how its forms of expression have changed in the course of history and what
kind of statement of belief would win general acceptance at
the present time.

Unfortunately it has at once to be admitted that those
outside the Christian faith must often find great difficulty in
determining what is a fair representation of essential
Christian doctrine. Systems of belief which men formulate
are always liable to become either too hard or too soft, too
rigid or too flabby. On the one side there has been the insis-
tence that a particular form of words must be accepted and
acknowledged as true by all those who desire to bear the
Christian name and to be admitted to full membership in the
Christian Church. A body of dogma is first defined and then
used as an ultimate test. All who are unwilling to subscribe
find themselves branded as unbelievers and regarded as outside the pale of the true Church. On the other side there has

been the easy-going assumption that no particular form of words is necessary to portray the Christian *spirit*. What matters is not words but deeds, not theory but practice. All who manifest a pattern of Christ-like behaviour have a right to be regarded as genuine members of the Christian Church.

These two extremes have been so widely held that they deserve to be examined a little more closely. The first looks for a solid foundation of *Dogma*. This need not necessarily be extended in its scope but it must be precise, unambiguous, final. Only with a firm dogmatic foundation, it is believed, can a strong and stable religious life be maintained. And indeed the foundation on which the Christian can build has been provided for him, it is said, by an original deposit of words corresponding exactly to the realities of the unique revelation of God in Christ.

This search for a dogmatic formulation arises partly out of the common human experience that a society if it is to be stable needs a formal constitution to provide rules and procedures for its government. But even more it springs from a deep-seated conviction that words can so be selected and structured together that the resultant formula will represent the ultimate truth of things in an exact statement. However far we may penetrate backwards into human history, verbal symbols have constituted man's chief instrument of communication and words have easily taken on a more-than-ordinary significance. When used to describe divine realities they have come to be regarded as taking on something of a divine quality themselves and therefore as needing to be treated with deference if not with reverence. A succinct statement about the nature and activity of God, if it once wins acceptance in a community, can easily take on a certain numinous quality. Henceforward it is sacrosanct, not to be tampered with, not to be changed. It is *dogma* and upon the foundation of unchanging dogma a Church can be securely built.

Such a view of dogma is in many ways attractive. It seems to offer stability, continuity, certainty. It seems to provide an altogether dependable link with the ultimate reality to which the dogma bears witness. But the fact remains that no pattern of words devised by man can possibly constitute an exact map of ultimate reality. Words themselves have to be translated into the languages of other cultures and in the very process become imprecise, uncertain, shifting. Even within a continuing cultural tradition life does not stand still and words gain ever new shades of meaning. A settled formula, a fixed dogma, cannot possibly serve for ever as an adequate representation of a living Reality. It can be of immense service in revealing the corporate conviction of a certain culture at a certain period of time. It squeezes the life out of religion if it comes to be regarded as an exact formula valid for all peoples and all times. In this book I shall try to treat the dogmatic formulations of the past with respect but I can never accord to them the status of final and infallible statements.

At the other extreme there is a view commonly held today that systems of belief are no longer really necessary. A sharp distinction is often drawn between doctrine and ethic. Doctrine, it is said, concerns matters which are quite beyond us. Its propositions cannot be proved either way: they may be right, they may be wrong. Why not abandon all attempts to express our relation to ultimate reality *in words* and concentrate instead on the ethical injunctions which have been left us by our Lord and by the apostles. These can be embodied in a general rule of conduct which, if obeyed, will lead the world forward to a better way of life.

Now in regard to this kind of plea two things it seems to me need to be said. First, nothing could be clearer from the New Testament than the fact that its ethic is derived directly from its doctrine. Jesus Himself came into Galilee proclaiming the nearness of God's reign and summoning men to turn and believe the good news. In other words His first concern was to make vividly clear to those who would listen the nature of God's activity and of His ultimate purpose. Parable after parable was designed to show men how God was at work in the world and how He was calling men to act in response to what He was doing. Moreover in the later part of the New Testament the sequence becomes even clearer. It is because of what God has done in sending His Son, it is because of the self-humiliation of the Christ to the death even of a cross, it is because of the outpouring of God's Spirit into our hearts—it is because of these great acts of God that we are called and challenged to behave in similar fashion. If God manifested His love, we ought to love one another. If Christ humbled Himself, we ought to serve one another. If the Spirit was given to inspire to holiness, we ought to walk in newness of life.

So far as the New Testament is concerned it would be unthinkable that its ethic could ever be divorced from its doctrine or that the one could be left vague and optional while the other was made clear-cut and obligatory. The Christian ethic is the corollary of Christian doctrine: Truth is in order to Goodness: it is in and through action that faith or belief reveals its true nature: these are affirmations altogether consonant with the spirit of the New Testament. But to imagine that men can construct programmes of social ethics worthy of the name Christian without any essential reference to the total revelation of God in Christ, which is the subject of Christian doctrine, is to be completely out of touch with the way in which the Christian movement has actually developed in the course of its history.

The second thing which needs to be said is that to set ethic before doctrine or exhortation to good action before the imaginative presentation of the nature of the good, is to go clean contrary to the order of things revealed to us through modern psychological investigation. Without attempting to divide up the human personality into separate compartments such as thought, emotion and will, it is at least possible to distinguish between the capacity on the one hand to perceive or imagine or envisage and on the other hand to resolve or commit oneself to a certain course of action. What is abundantly clear in the realm of human behaviour is that the first of these capacities is the more important and influential of the two. A man may for example envisage a pattern of life in which he sees the possibility of a rich satisfaction of his inner desires and a likely fulfilment of his own personality. In contrast to this a different pattern of action is urged upon him as being perhaps his duty to society or as bringing perhaps immediate external rewards. If his imagination has really been captured by the first, then no amount of exhortation or threatening or cajoling in relation to the second is likely to have much effect upon his conduct.

So it follows that if Christian doctrine can be presented to the imagination vividly and comprehensively and in forms which are all the time related to the human situation, the effect in terms of producing the Christian way of life is likely to be far greater than would follow from the proclamation of Christian ethical precepts in isolation. The results which follow from direct exhortation or from concentration upon particular Christian duties are often disappointingly small. It is when the ethic is envisaged within the total context of the Christian revelation—and it is with this that Christian doctrine is concerned—it is then that man is most likely to respond in such a way as to bring his own pattern of life into conformity with that of the Divine.

So in my approach to Christian doctrine I shall seek to avoid on the one side the precise and unyielding dogmatic formulation, on the other side the vague and emasculated ethical exhortation. I shall attempt rather to present the Christian revelation as a comprehensive whole, to be apprehended by the human imagination under different forms, all of which have their part to play in bearing witness to the transcendent wonder of the Being and Activity of God Himself.

II

I have referred to the difficulty which those outside the Christian faith often experience of determining what are the essential beliefs of Christianity. I should like now to state as clearly as I can what is the central subject of our concern in this book. Obviously we are not starting our enquiry with a completely blank sheet. Something is already there in

the total Christian tradition offering itself for our considera-
tion. There are, in fact, many things in the tradition which
are worthy of attention but at the heart of all and at the
source of all is the majestic confession of the living God,
Father, Son and Holy Spirit. Whether we look to the New
Testament or to the early Fathers or to the great mediaeval
philosopher-theologians or to the Reformers or to modern
exponents of the faith this at least we find to be a common
element in their testimony: that the God whom they worship and to whom they seek to bear witness is a God who is
known in a threefold way as Father, Son and Holy Spirit.

Let us look for a moment at the New Testament. No one
reading this collection of writings could easily deny that the
authors, however varied they may be in other ways, all
share the deep conviction that their whole existence
depends upon the purpose and providence and good
pleasure of the living God. He is before them both in the
history of their fathers and in their own individual histories.
He is above them both in the over-arching providence of the
natural order and in the care of every one of His creatures.
He is beyond them both in the destiny planned for all
humanity and in the future lot appointed for every child of
man. We might express their general outlook by saying that
they were deeply conscious of the fact that their existence
as human beings was *bounded* but that beyond the boundary
in every direction was, not an empty nothingness, but the
constant concern and activity of the living God Himself.

Now it is true that this conviction would have been in
large measure shared by the prophets and psalmists of the
Old Testament period. But something revolutionary had
happened before the New Testament writings began to be

circulated. According to their unanimous testimony, a Divine Being had come into the very midst of men's earthly existence. He had taken indeed the form of a servant. He had appeared in ordinary human guise. He had gone about doing good. But the consensus of testimony is clear. This Jesus was Emmanuel—God with us. He was the Word, the only-begotten, dwelling among us. He was God manifest in the flesh—born of David's seed by natural descent but declared Son of God with power when He was raised from the dead. This general outlook we might describe by saying that men had become deeply conscious of the fact that God had pierced through the boundary of their existence, not simply by the speaking of a word or by the performance of a dramatic act, but by an actual coming in personal presence to visit and redeem His people. Whatever else needed to be said about the career of Jesus this must be affirmed without qualification: that this career was a direct revelation in the midst of human life of the personal presence and purposeful activity of the living God Himself.

But even this was not all. The incarnate son of God might have come into the world and dwelt amongst men and been raised again to the glory of the Father. This in itself would have been a unique wonder but it would not have dealt directly with the total human situation. So we find a further testimony, deeply impressive by reason of the fact that it is an obvious interpretation of living experience. The Divine Spirit—and God Himself is Spirit—had actually entered into the inmost shrines of human personalities. He had come as the fire, cleansing the inner springs: He had come as the wind, renewing the energies: He had come as the breath, bringing healing and peace. So within the collective structure of the interior life of the community, God Himself had been actively working. Within the individual human heart, God's touch had been felt. This new outlook we might describe by saying that men were deeply conscious of the fact that the living God had actually communicated His personal spirit into the inmost structures of corporate and individual life. This was not just an occasional stimulus to sanctity or a periodic inflow of new energy. The God of the Beyond, Who had revealed Himself in the Here and Now, had extended that revelation into the hidden realm of the human personality and that presence in the interior of human life was to be an abiding presence.

God Who is forever over us and beyond us is the God Who has come into our immediate environment and into our historic existence between past and future. Furthermore, God Who is over us and amongst us is the God Who has graciously penetrated the world of instincts, emotions, desires, motives, intentions, relationships which constitute the inward dimension of human existence. In simplest terms the New Testament writers shared a common faith in a God Who is beyond all earthly limitations and yet has lived as man within these limitations: a faith too in a God Who stands over against man and yet has communicated Himself into the very inner consciousness of man. God beyond us: God for us: God within us: this is the God to Whom the New Testament bears witness and Who is the subject of all Christian doctrinal formulations.

The general witness of the New Testament is entirely confirmed when we examine the way in which creeds developed in the early Church. A very long time would elapse before any kind of fixity or uniformity could be established in the Church though ultimately two out-standing patterns—the Western represented by what today we call the Apostles' Creed and the Eastern represented by what we call the Nicene—gained wide acceptance. But at a very early stage threefold confession was adopted and it seems to have been a common practice at the initiation ceremony to baptize the candidate three times. While he stood in the water he was asked three successive questions concerning his belief in Father, Son and Holy Spirit. After each affirmative reply he was plunged into the water and after the third his baptism was complete. Even in the 2nd century, before any explicit reference to a formal con-fession of faith appears, we find Justin Martyr describing a baptism ceremony in which the candidates "receive a lustral washing in the water in the name of the Father and Lord God of the universe and of our Saviour Jesus Christ and of the Holy Spirit". And by the beginning of the third century the answers of the candidates to the threefold interrogations are approximating very closely to the three clauses of what we now call the Apostles' Creed.

It is true that the New Testament shows evidence that in the earliest days of the Church's missionary activity a can-didate for baptism might only be asked to confess Jesus as the Christ or as Son of God: or he might be required to learn a twofold confession by which he acknowledged the Father as source of all and the Son as agent of all. But taking the New Testament as a whole, the Trinitarian reference is unmistakable and this threefold pattern estab-lished itself more and more firmly as the creeds of the Church approached a settled uniformity.

The wondering confession of faith in the living God,

Father, Son and Holy Spirit has retained its central position in the Church's doctrine and liturgy throughout the centuries. Among all who profess and call themselves Christians the dominant subject of Christian doctrine has been the living God, Father, Son and Holy Spirit. In prayer and praise men have addressed Him as such: in systems of doctrine men have interpreted Him as such. It will be our task now to attempt a fresh interpretation of what this faith means and implies in the context of our lives today.

Chapter Two

THE HUMAN SITUATION

EVERY age seems to produce its own particular crop of key-words. A word which may have played a modest part in a language-system over a long period suddenly becomes prominent and finds itself constantly in use. Such a word in our own time is 'relevant' or its antithesis 'irrelevant'. If a theme or a question can be dismissed as irrelevant that is the end of the matter. Life is too short, it is inferred, to play about with irrelevancies. What bearing has the theme proposed for discussion upon the actualities of everyday life? What relation has any particular pronouncement to questions which people are really asking?

This temper of the world at large is one which the Christian theologian cannot afford to ignore. There may be occasions when doctrines whose relevance to modern life and its problems may not be immediately obvious can be expounded because of their sheer historic interest or even because it is assumed that they are of permanent significance although their relation to contemporary problems may not appear on the surface. But in the main it is the task of the Christian interpreter today to show that the central confession of his faith *is* relevant to the needs of humanity whether these be considered from the individual or from the corporate point of view.

The all-important matter therefore which we need first to

determine is whether men are asking questions today to which the Christian faith in God, Father, Son and Holy Spirit, provides any kind of reply. Or to put it in another way, have the investigations of artists, psychologists, historians and sociologists into the human condition uncovered basic needs which characterize man's life at all times and in all places and to which the Christian faith is clearly relevant? Relatedness and relevancy are from one angle dangerous concepts for it is always open to the critic to affirm that the answer simply arises out of the question or that the proposed supply is simply the projection of the need. Yet the danger from another angle is even greater. To propound Christian dogmas without any kind of reference to man's questionings or to obvious human needs is to speak into emptiness and to gain the response only of the echo of one's own voice. Recognizing the reality of the first danger it is my own intention to expose myself to it rather than to reiterate orthodoxy in terms which bear little relation to my own understanding of the human situation.

To give in brief compass a comprehensive survey of human life, its needs and its questions, its anxieties and its hopes, is as daunting an enterprise as could well be imagined. So vast a quantity of evidence is now at our disposal. The sheer bulk of material made available by the historian over the past 150 years is far too great for any single mind to encompass. The violent controversies among social scientists since the days of Marx concerning the proper pattern of the political and economic life of the community tend to leave the ordinary individual in a state of bewilderment. The psychologist's combination of voluminous data derived from observation of human behaviour with wide-ranging speculation and theorizing about the processes of man's unconscious mind gives the layman at the present time little opportunity to speak confidently about the structure of the human personality. Yet in spite of the great difficulties attendant upon any attempt to analyse man's nature and developing condition in any inclusive way, I still propose to set him within a fourfold framework which, so far as I can judge, is compatible with the general conclusions of a wide body of informed opinion at the present time.

Man, it seems to me, is constantly concerned with four clamant questions.

1. *The question of security*

From start to finish man's life is insecure. How can he be assured of physical security—of breath, of food, of drink, of shelter, of protection, of a suitable environment for the propagation of his species? Still more, how can he be assured of personal security—of the presence of the mother, of the strength of the father, of acceptance by the wider group, of the establishment and continuance of individual identity? A child at the very beginning is helpless and yet is acutely aware of certain conditions which provide a feeling of comfort, of others which produce intolerable discomfort. To be comfortable is to be secure and vice versa. And the source of all comfort and all security in the very earliest stages is without doubt the mother herself.

The mother provides food, the mother ensures warmth, she watches against all hindrances to easy breathing, she keeps the infant dry and clean. Still more she becomes, at least ideally, the personal environment of the child, responding to its cries of pain and recognizing its smiles of

29

pleasure. Still further she looks to the future, anticipating the child's development and planning accordingly. So dependent is the child on the mother that, as John Macmurray has pointed out, every call for the mother springs out of a fear of isolation and since isolation if it lasts too long means death, this is implicitly a sign of the fear of death.[1]

Security therefore is from the first built upon the relation between the child and the mother. There can, of course, be maternal substitutes. To quote from Macmurray's valuable chapter on Mother and Child "The term 'mother' . . . is not a biological term. It means simply the adult who cares for the baby. Usually it will be the woman who bore him, but this is not necessarily so. A human infant does not necessarily die, like an animal, if his mother dies in child-birth. The mother may be an aunt, or an elder sister or a hired nurse. She need not even be a female. A man can do all the mothering that is necessary if he is provided with a feeding bottle, and learns how to do it in precisely the same fashion that a woman must learn."[2] Whether or not this optimistic estimate of a man's capabilities is justified the root principle carries unqualified psychological support: the principle namely that all security in life rests upon some maternal matrix and that without this sense of basic trust in a gracious protecting environment no individual can attain confidence or stability.

The maternal matrix of which I have just spoken may be extended in more than one direction. It may for example be extended to the section of the natural environment over which the mother holds sway. This may be a single-roomed

1 *Persons in Relation*, p. 62
2 *Ibid*, p. 50

hut, an enclosure, a mansion —within this particular area the individual is conscious of the familiar and the secure. Or it may be extended symbolically as the mother creates an artificial framework of sights and sounds which gradually become familiar to the child. Language and music, rituals of eating and drinking, furnishings and decoration, all can serve as extensions of the mother's own personality and consequently as parts of a symbolic maternal matrix of security.

A still wider extension of maternal security appears when we examine the elementary forms of social life disclosed to us by the researches of anthropologists and sociologists. The simplest form of tribal life resembles that of a large family and security is found by remaining within the bounds of what might be described as home territory. This territory provides food and drink and easily comes to be regarded as the earth-mother. To preserve its fertility, to protect it from desecration, is the sacred duty of those who depend upon it for their continuing life. So 'The Land' takes on mystic significance as the place of security and identity and a particular tribal group becomes restless and afraid if the bonds binding it to the earth-mother are broken. Thus in the experience of the individual, the family, the tribe, the nation, a mother-figure is essential. Only when there is relationship to some kind of maternal matrix—and this principle applies not only to early and formative years—can there be security and abiding trust.

2. *The question of freedom*

The immediate paradox confronts us that although man has at all times been concerned with the question of security, he has through large sections of his history been concerned also with the question of freedom. From the helplessness of infancy the child moves forward to the stage of expanding his range of activities and feeling the development of his own powers. He begins to experiment with arms and hands, legs and feet, tongue and throat, all the time testing his own capacities and seeking a wider freedom. He will have many frustrations and even failures and the temptation will constantly arise to withdraw into the familiar security and to remain within the maternal nest. In fact if man were a being conditioned solely by his experiences of the expanding world he might well be induced to give up the struggle and to remain within the limited circle of the cosy and the comfortable. But something drives him forward and compels him to ask the question of freedom again and again. The expanding horizon is just as necessary as the maternal matrix.

In this effort to expand, the individual is concerned not only with the settled world of impersonal structures in which he has hitherto lived—how he is to move beyond them—but also with a world of persons of whom he becomes increasingly aware. The person who can do effectually what he himself is seeking to do painfully is the object of admiration and it may be of envy and jealousy. Ambivalent feelings stir in his heart. He seeks to follow and to emulate the successful pioneer whom he has watched admiringly. At the same time he seeks to surpass or to overcome the rival who in any way interferes with his own progress. Freedom is thus a double-sided phenomenon, sometimes directed towards future expansion and achievement, sometimes set towards the overcoming of entanglements inherited from the past. There is no longer the relative simplicity of the maternal situation. Freedom will almost certainly depend not only upon devotion to the shining example of the deliverer but also upon denial of the claims of those who seek to defend the closed patterns of the past.

The struggle for freedom, whether on the part of the individual or of the band of brothers or of the revolutionary faction in a society, never ceases. Indeed the history of mankind itself has been written in terms of an ever-increasing effort to gain an ever-widening freedom. For history, as it has come to be known and described in the past two centuries, has necessarily focussed attention upon significant events and critical exploits and striking changes in the pattern of human life. Wherever an individual or a society stays within a well-defined area and moves according to a well-defined rhythm of existence, history is scarcely in the making. The regular pattern can be described but that is all. History is concerned with the man who, for no immediately obvious reason, went out from the settled and familiar, not knowing whither he went. It is concerned with the band of slaves who, having been stirred to action by the example of a revolutionary leader, broke loose from their bondage and set out upon their journey over the trackless desert to the promised land.

It is a far cry from the child of six or seven years old, testing its own powers in a simple venture beyond the confines of some familiar security, to the astronaut of middle age who commits himself to a complex adventure into space beyond the limits of any experience hitherto known. Yet the basic motivation is the same. Since first a living human being broke through the bounds of the safe and secure and ventured out into the unknown, freedom, so to speak, has been

33

in the blood. The urge is there and it cannot be denied. The adventure is a breaking with the familiar and must always therefore involve the overcoming of powers, personal and impersonal, which incarnate the bounded in space and the past in time. But it is also a breaking through into the unfamiliar and must always therefore see the advent of a new man, a hero, a leader, a deliverer. The 'free' man leads his brothers into 'freedom'—this is part of the continuing pattern of human life and unless man brings history to an end by settling for the comforts of a totally mechanized existence the question of freedom will never receive a final answer.

3. *The question of order*

Whereas human history can be viewed as a succession of struggles for enlargement and for a wider exercise of freedom, it can also with equal justification be viewed as a continuing search for just order. Nothing is clearer than that man grows weary of confusion, arbitrariness, uncertainty, above all of anarchy. He may catch the vision of a way of escape from restrictions and oppressions which he finds galling and humiliating. He breaks out from the yoke of bondage into some new area of freedom and for a time is sustained by the sense of achievement and of common destiny. But sooner or later the often unpalatable truth has to be accepted—that freedom without order, heroic defiance without voluntary discipline, are of only transitory value. A state of affairs in which every man tends to do that which is right in his own eyes is less to be desired than that in which the individual is required to conform to laws which are at least designed for the good of the whole.

34

How often in history has the revolution, carried through with so great enthusiasm, been succeeded by disillusionment, contraction, sectional quarrellings and personal rivalries! How often has man had to learn the bitter lesson that freedom can never be finally won under the conditions of earthly limitations! That which is gained through struggle must be conserved through a new ordering of society. Treachery must be succeeded by co-operation, lawlessness by freely accepted laws, fighting for a limited objective by the constructive upbuilding of a new régime. The cry of the Old Testament warrior "Shall the sword slay for ever?" has echoed down through the centuries and has symbolized the weariness which settles upon those who see no way of establishing a stable order.

Not that it is ever possible to make a clear-cut separation between the struggle for freedom and the establishment of order. Often the very strength of the pattern of discipline accepted by the liberating agents in the course of their struggle makes it possible for a minimum basis of order to be immediately available for the new society. Or a remarkably well-ordered community may already be in existence before the struggle begins which is designed to remove the pressure of an extraneous power at certain vital points. Recent discoveries on the shores of the Dead Sea have shown that the ill-fated rebellion of Bar-Cochba and his followers was engineered out of the very midst of a society which readily accepted the most intricate disciplines in matters of land-tenure and water-supply. The struggle was designed to remove pressures which were offensive, not to open a door to licence and anarchy. A still more famous example of the dialectical interplay of freedom and order is to be found in the story of Luther's struggle for the realization of the liberty of a Christian man, soon to be followed by the struggle of the peasants for a kind of liberty which Luther could in no way approve.

One of the outstanding symbols of order in the history of mankind is the city. The family and the tribe are *natural* associations. Even the dissident group which struggles for new freedom, though quickened for a particular task by a common purpose, is likely to have an already existing unity dependent upon blood-relationship. But a city comes into being as the result of a will to ordered living. People from varying backgrounds elect to live within an artificial enclosure under rules concerning housing, communications, food supplies, health, cleanliness, property, which are often of a most complex kind. Indeed the multiplication of laws for expanding and developing cities has become one of the almost frightening phenomena of the twentieth century. Yet people are willing to have their freedom of movement curbed at innumerable points so long as they can be assured of dependable regularities in what are regarded as the essentials of civilized life.

In this quest for order one other point stands out clearly. For the framing and administering and adjusting of laws there must be personal agents who are themselves men of integrity and discipline. The civilized world looks back upon a long succession of law-givers, judges, teachers of the law, interpreters of the law, framers of new constitutions, guardians of the peace, all of whom are dedicated ideally to the task of providing and preserving a stable framework within which men may go about their ordinary lawful pursuits unhindered and unharmed. The more the world has contracted, the more complex this framework has become. But man must have such a framework unless he is to return to the atmosphere of the jungle and renounce civilized life as an end in which he has lost all interest.

4. *The question of meaning*

Perhaps the strangest fact of all in man's developing history is that he has never for long been satisfied with the attainment of any or all of the goods which we have already considered. There may be the most ample sense of security in a paradisiac situation and still man wants to break out and experiment and explore. There may be the most exhilarating sense of involvement in the campaign which will bring release from bondage and direct men's steps towards the promised land and still there will be the concern for the establishment of orderliness and a measure of restraint. There may be the most satisfying sense of being members of an ordered and well-disciplined society and still men will ask: "What does it all mean?"

The question of meaning, to be sure, arises in many forms. The scientist as he examines the pattern of human evolution may ask about its inner dynamic and whether in fact the process is moving towards a goal. The artist, as he works on his forms and perfects his techniques can hardly avoid asking from time to time about inner content and the way in which this is being interpreted. The worker in a great industry must sometimes wonder whether there is nothing more to be concerned about than efficient production and equitable distribution. The rulers of cities recognize that it is not sufficient for a body corporate to be sustained solely on the physical level but that it needs the cohesion which can only be gained by recognizing that all activities have a part to play in the unfolding of the significance of the whole.

The human institution which has symbolized this search for meaning, coherence, integration, wisdom, has been the university. Its very name relates it to that which is universal. Its activities, carried on in many different departments, ideally focus attention upon one question: Is there any single meaning to this whole vast mass of accumulated knowledge? Or to put it in another way. When the world of nature and the long record of history have yielded up their secrets and these have been carefully stored and tabulated, do they include anything distinctive which can constitute a principle of integration and therefore an indicator of meaning?

It is indeed true that the notion of meaning is exceedingly difficult to track down and define. The question of the meaning of meaning easily emerges and soon we are launched on an infinite regress. But however the matter may be discussed in theory and logic, it remains true that man as man has the power of distinguishing between that which is meaningful and that which is senseless, that which has shape and that which is formless. In the simplest patterns of speech and symbolism, words and shapes lock into one another in such a way that a tentative wholeness becomes apparent. And man gains a mysterious satisfaction in recognizing the most elementary pattern of wholeness. So he continues to stretch out and embrace more and more of life's objects and experiences, always with the hope of discovering a richer integration within a more meaningful whole.

This fourth question about meaning is most obviously the

one which can never be finally answered. But in point of fact none of the questions which I have framed can receive final solutions as long as life endures. Life can never be finally encapsulated within formal categories. At every stage, each of the questions comes up for reconsideration as man recapitulates in some way an experience through which he passed at an earlier period in his own development. The distinguishing of the four, therefore, is not intended to be in any way a rigid separation of the four, each from the other, in isolated compartments. The four are inter-related in the most fascinating and wonderful way. Their importance for our purpose is that they give us the living situations, the contextual frameworks, the patterns of language, the names and symbols, through which we can try to interpret the significance of the fundamental Christian confession of faith.

In concluding this chapter I return to the key-word with which I began. The Christian faith in God, Father, Son and Holy Spirit can only be seen as *relevant* to man's abiding condition if it can be expressed in terms related to his abiding needs. To gauge the nature of these needs our most valuable index is the character of the questions he asks. If then we are right in defining the questions of security, freedom, order and meaning as all-important and in a certain sense as all-inclusive, then our only hope of interpreting Christian doctrine relevantly is to apply the faith to each of the four patterns of recurring need and to see where this leads us. This I shall now attempt to do.

Chapter Three

THE FAMILY OF GOD

THE Christian responds in faith to the God Who, though for ever beyond us, has yet come near us and even dwells within us. Let us now try to interpret this faith in terms of those images and relationships which have become most widely familiar during the course of human history.

I

First there is the family and the home. The simplest form of social organization is that of a kin-group, occupying a limited area of space, provided with some kind of rudimentary shelter and protection and presided over by a parent-figure who may be male or female. Out of this characteristic situation man's earliest images are born. In particular the imagery of the life of religion draws upon family relationships and experiences so that it is common in primitive religions to find references to the Earth Mother or to the Sky-Father, to families of gods and divine beings, to spirits of the home or hearth, to the giving of life in order that life may be sustained or renewed. Security and stability are found under the care of a family deity who must receive due honour and obedience and whose life must be maintained through regular gifts and offerings.

Though the revelation of God to which the Bible bears

witness rises far above these primitive conceptions yet the imagery of family and home is neither rejected nor abandoned. The quest for security is recognized to be legitimate and the assurance is given again and again that the only foundation for confident living is to be found in the fatherly care of God Himself. He is the source and begetter of all life and it is unthinkable that He who begets life will not also protect and sustain it and bring it to its true fulfilment. Such a faith is to be found in the Old Testament as well as in the New. But the New Testament advances beyond the Old. It affirms that the life itself was manifested in human terms within a particular historical career. This life was the untainted image of the Divine original: it maintained its integrity unspoiled throughout the course of its human embodiment. Still further the New Testament affirms that the revelation of this life in space and time made possible the emergence of a new humanity, a humanity cleansed, revivified, and re-created in the same basic pattern.

To express the matter thus is to stay largely within the compass of the abstract and the impersonal. But the Biblical writers are rarely content with merely general ideas. They seek constantly to record God's dealings with men in terms of the *personal*. So the Bible gives body to the affirmations which I have just outlined by expressing them in terms of a family existence in which ideally all life begins, continues and ends in the exercise of mutual love. The ultimate source of human security and identity, it says, is the electing love of God the Father: the ultimate assurance of this electing love is the incarnation of God the Son: the ultimate experience of this love is through the fellowship of

41

God the Holy Spirit. This is the Christian faith expressed in terms of home and family and we are now ready to look more closely at the way in which the Bible expands this imagery. But before doing so it may be well to look squarely at one difficulty which arises when we use the relationships of home and family to interpret Christian doctrine.

Why, it may be asked, has Christian doctrine virtually excluded the mother-figure from its total imagery of family relationships as applied to God and His dealings with mankind? Is it not evident that amongst peoples the world over it has seemed natural to think of the Divine in terms of the mother? Is it not also clear that the general tendency of the human heart is to envisage a framework of security in maternal rather than in paternal terms—the mother supreme in the home, the mother-land, mother-church and so on? Has not the absence of the feminine from the accepted imagery of the Divine encouraged the surreptitious introduction of devotion to the feminine-principle in often undesirable ways?

That there is point in these questions cannot be denied. Judaism and its offshoots, Christianity and Islam, have often tended to give a quite undue prominence to the masculine principle within their conceptions of the Deity. Particularly is this true of Judaism and Islam and certain sections of Reformed Christendom. So exalted a place has been accorded to the male in the social structure that it has seemed natural to attribute not only masculine names but also dominantly masculine qualities to the Deity. But although this may be readily admitted, it does not follow that it would be any more desirable to revert to what was common, for example, in the ancient Mediterranean world and to apply to the Deity names and characteristics which are dominantly feminine instead.

Modern biological and psychological studies have shown that the sharp distinction between male and female which was generally assumed as recently as a century ago cannot any longer be sustained. In any male, feminine elements are to be found and vice versa. It would indeed be possible to express this imaginatively by constructing some kind of androgynous figure but the result is bound to be artificial for in fact no precise balancing or merging of the two sets of characteristics is possible in human life. There may have been an attempt by the priestly author of Genesis 1 to approximate to this idea in his claim that God created man in his own image, "male and female created he them" (1 . 27). But the Old Testament does not pursue the matter further. Rather it frankly speaks of the Deity in masculine terms and leaves us in no doubt that as in Hebrew society the father was head of the family so in the Divine order of things God is best spoken of within the same pattern of imagery.

As I have already suggested, this adoption of the masculine appellation led in some aspects of Hebrew religion and later in Islam to an extreme concentration upon isolated and exaggerated masculine qualities. But this was not the case in the Old Testament taken as a whole and certainly not in the New Testament. Fatherhood includes qualities of mercy and forgiveness, tenderness and gentleness, care and sustenance, concern for safety and comfort and renewal of life. It is particularly noticeable moreover that there is never any emphasis upon the sexual qualities of the male when masculine names or titles are applied to the Deity. If we

43

envisage the total family complex without isolating or emphasizing unduly the particular sexual characteristics of any member of it, then the imagery of fatherhood and sonship seems entirely appropriate. No pattern of imagery taken from human experience can be entirely adequate to describe Divine relationships and activities. But to use the father-son imagery within the context of a total family-context is, it seems to me, legitimate as a means of interpreting the relevance of the Christian faith to the basic needs of human nature.[1]

II

In the experience of a normal family no event is more eagerly anticipated or more excitingly welcomed than the birth of a child. The emergence of new life anywhere is of considerable moment but nothing really compares with the mysterious process by which a woman, having endured the long strain of pregnancy and the sharp pains of childbirth, sets forward a new life upon its individual way. Many are the explanations which man has devised to account for this extraordinary phenomenon. For long the question was what had entered into the woman to bring about so amazing a result. Had she imbibed some powerful force from the neighbourhood of one of the holy places? Had she received a spirit from one of the deceased ancestors of the tribe? There was the mystery of the creation of the tiny body. There was also the mystery of the soul or spirit which had made this body its habitation.

Gradually the part which man played in the procreative

[1] Cf. G. van der Leeuw, *Religion in Essence and Manifestation*, pp. 99-100

act came to be known and woman's dependence upon the gift of man's seed was recognized. But still the question about the origin of the soul or spirit of life remained unanswered. Did this come from some supernatural source? Was it specially created for the individual in question? Or was the soul indestructible and transmissible from one body to another? These questions have fascinated men everywhere though perhaps they interested the Hebrews less than most. For them all that seems to have finally mattered was the faith that man's physical frame had been fashioned by God Himself and that his soul was a direct gift from the same source. "The Lord God formed man of dust from the ground, and breathed into his nostrils the breath of life; and man became a living being" (Gen. 2. 7. R.S.V.).

In the Old Testament no use is made of imagery drawn from the begetting of children within the natural order to describe God's relations with mankind at large. Instead the father-son relationship is reserved for God's relation to Israel and to Israel's anointed king. And even Israel had no right to assume the enjoyment of such a relationship by virtue of any natural genealogy or physical birth. Israel's only justification for regarding God as father was that He in His pure graciousness had looked favourably upon His people and called them into a relationship comparable to that of a father with a son. In fact God had loved this family, had called it to Himself, had watched over it and guarded it, had patiently borne with its faults and failings, had forgiven its shortcomings, had refused to abandon it when it had virtually forsaken Him. Yet from the Old Testament writings we can derive no comprehensive doctrine of the fatherhood of God. In the occasional inspired utterance of prophet and

45

psalmist we see the Divine pity and generosity such as a father or mother might show towards an erring child being manifested towards Israel—but that is all. It is to other patterns of imagery that we must look if we are to discover the characteristic emphases of the Old Testament witness to the living God.

It is true that in the late Wisdom writings and in the teaching of the rabbis it was customary to address God as Father but still the reference was strictly confined to the care of and special concern for Israel. This makes it all the more striking that the New Testament abounds in references to father-son and family imagery and in the Fourth Gospel the relation of the Father to the Son may be said to constitute the controlling theme of the whole book. We shall therefore try to see how the central Christian faith in God, Father, Son and Holy Spirit is unfolded in the New Testament by means of the use of the imagery of the home.

III

Let me begin by quoting a striking statement from Frederick C. Grant's *Introduction to New Testament Thought.*

"If one wishes to feel the very pulse beat of any high religion, it must as a rule be sought in its liturgy."

This I am sure is profoundly true. It is doubtless important to study the writings of theologians who have attempted to express their own apprehension of the nature and activity of God in clear and balanced language. It may be even more important to study the prayers, individual and corporate, of those who have tried to express this apprehension through worthy forms of devotion.

We cannot, of course, expect to find highly developed liturgies in New Testament times—the surprising thing is that there are so many evidences to show that creeds and set patterns of prayer were already beginning to take shape. Of these there is, in my judgment, none more significant than that which is repeated three times in exactly the same form (once in a letter of St. Paul, once in a Pauline encyclical and once in a Petrine Epistle) and referred to in a worship-passage in the Epistle to the Romans. This is the formula:

"Blessed be the God and Father of our Lord Jesus Christ".

In one case this is expanded and applied to those in sorrow and affliction: the Father of our Lord Jesus Christ is the Father of mercies and of all comfort. In a second case it is applied to those who had been in a state of spiritual poverty and dereliction: the Father of our Lord Jesus Christ supplies unlimited spiritual blessings to those in need. In the third case it is applied to those who had been aliens from the heavenly commonwealth, a people without identity or expectancy: the Father of our Lord Jesus Christ begets them again to a living hope and assures them of an imperishable destiny. Finally in the Romans passage believers are exhorted with one voice to glorify "the God and Father of our Lord Jesus Christ".

But this is not the only evidence to show how prominent a place the name 'Father' held in early Christian prayer. In the Epistle to the Galatians St. Paul reminds his converts that God had sent the Spirit of His Son into their hearts leading them to cry out "Abba, Father". And again in the Epistle to the Romans he affirms that the prayer-cry "Abba,

Father" is the outward evidence of the Spirit's witness with our spirit that we are children of God. Only on one other occasion can this combination "Abba, Father" be found in the New Testament and that is in the record of the agony in the Garden of Gethsemane. Then Jesus cries: "Abba, Father, everything is possible for thee: let this cup pass from me. Yet not my will but thine be done." At the same time it is not only possible but probable that the prayer which Jesus taught His disciples and which has come down to us with the opening words "Our Father" actually began, when originally given, with this same word "Abba", the intimate address to the Father-God.

The doctrinal importance of these prayer-fragments can hardly be over-emphasized. They show that when hearts were soaring in praise and thanksgiving for the new life which had come to men through Jesus Christ, the natural form of expression was to ascribe glory to the God and Father of our Lord Jesus Christ. As Father He had bestowed upon the Beloved Son the wealth of His love, His comfort, His heavenly kingdom. But that which had been given to the Son had through the Spirit been bestowed also upon those who had been called into sonship. That God is the bountiful, generous, compassionate, life-giving Father is the unmistakable implication of the majestic liturgical blessings which these early documents contain. In addition, however, there are the familiar, intimate, almost childlike cries "Abba, Father". They show that in joy and in sorrow, in the quiet of confidence and in the strain of conflict, in the moment of new revelation and in the regular routine of daily life, it was natural, in the fellowship of Jesus Christ, to say "Father". That God is the altogether sympathetic and understanding, while at the same time the bracing and challenging and even all-demanding 'Father' is the inescapable implication of these utterly spontaneous and heartfelt entreaties. I doubt if anything is clearer in the witness of the New Testament than that Jesus Himself addressed God regularly and persistently as 'Father' and that His early disciples, conscious of their new filial dignity, addressed God in similar fashion as Father or as Father of our Lord Jesus Christ.

But it is impossible to ascribe glory and blessing to an all-beneficent Father or to direct entreaties to an all-challenging Father unless there is the profound sense that the Father so addressed is beyond, transcendent, other than ourselves in the core of His personal existence. Jesus, having come amongst men and elected to share their lot, related Himself to God in the way that men must also relate themselves if they are to experience reality. God as Father is the Father in heaven or the heavenly Father: He is the source and giver of all that is good: He is at the same time the one who calls for unreserved commitment to His purpose of forgiveness and reconciliation. His generosity shames us: His call to reconciliation daunts us: He is far, far beyond any imaginable earthly father and yet He is still 'Father'. He is Father as revealed in the life and testimony of the true son, Jesus Christ. No man knoweth the Father save the Son and he to whom the Son willeth to reveal Him.

IV

Continuing within the context of family relationships our next enquiry concerns the nature and status of man himself. Has it been the Christian assumption that all men everywhere are to be regarded as children of God but that those who have entered into a relationship with the perfect Son are thereby set apart, as it were, into a special category? Or is the assumption rather that those who are outside the specifically Christian family have no right to be regarded as children—that they are without God in their earthly existence and without hope of any new quality of life beyond the grave? These are extraordinarily difficult questions to answer with any confidence. It has often been pointed out that there is no direct reference in the New Testament to God as the father of all men with the possible exception of Paul's quotation from the heathen poet in his address at Athens ("We are indeed His offspring"). This does not mean however that men at large are to be regarded as outside the bounds of the Divine care and concern. That those who have become united through faith with the Son of God's love are in a quite special sense sons or children of God—of this there can be no doubt. But as touching the rest of mankind it is dangerous to speak dogmatically on the basis of the Biblical evidence alone.

The matter is complicated so far as the New Testament is concerned by reason of the special status accorded to Israel, the chosen people of God. None of the apostolic writers doubted that those who were Hebrews according to the flesh were members of a family which had been given a special mission by God to bring blessing to the whole earth. Those who belonged to this family (and it was possible for an outsider to be incorporated into this family by special rites and instructions) were in a quite definite sense children of Abraham by natural descent, children of God by a heavenly calling and adoption. But the constant problem confronting spiritually sensitive souls in Israel was that of the instability and defection and even apostasy of their own fellow countrymen. Was a point ever reached when a man had so forfeited his birthright that he could no longer lay claim to any inheritance in the family of God? And those who were content to remain on a low level of moral attainment—how could they be aroused to seek their true standing as children of God?

Furthermore there was the question of those outside the covenant and the promises, those who, so far as fleshly descent was concerned, had no right to call upon God as their Father. Were they altogether excluded from the Divine favour? Or was it possible that they had a certain status within the Divine family as slaves even though they did not qualify as sons? And if they were nothing more than servants, how could they gain the status of sons? These were the problems and questions which constantly engaged the attention of early Christian witnesses and there were no simple and immediate answers. It was only as the full implications of the revelation in Christ, the perfect Son, became clear that a doctrine of man and his relation to God began to be formulated.

For what had been the teaching of Jesus Himself? As we read the first three gospels we gradually distinguish four main classes of men. There were the religious leaders who were often self-righteous and concerned with detailed rules of behaviour rather than with living personal faith: there were the uneducated masses who though ignorant of the law often displayed a remarkable depth of personal religion: there were the publicans and sinners who though technically within the racial boundary had virtually excluded themselves from the covenant privileges: and there were the outsiders, the Gentiles, who had no place in the Divine family although they sometimes showed themselves astonishingly alive to spiritual values. With all of these groups Jesus was in touch and it is important to notice His attitude to each.

For the scribes and Pharisees, hypocrites, Jesus had scathing words of denunciation. God's favour is not to be won by patterns of legal exactitude. They were excluding themselves from membership in God's true family. For the poor in spirit and the humble of heart Jesus had words of strong encouragement. God's good will is assured to those who hunger and thirst after better things: He constantly watches over the least of His children. For the publicans and sinners Jesus had a great compassion. He went to them, ate and drank with them, identified Himself with them and declared by word and deed that they could be restored to their rightful position as sons of God. Once and for all the story of the prodigal has shown that no son ever strays outside the range of the Father's love: once and for all the record of Zacchaeus has shown that God's own Son came to seek and to save the sons who, according to the religious standards of their day, had been given up as lost. It was the publican who went down to his house justified. It was the penitent thief who was assured of a place in the heavenly paradise.

But still there were those beyond the bounds of Israel — the Gentiles who knew not God. Here we must frankly admit that there is little direct evidence on which to build definite conclusions. Jesus by His own confession saw His ministry as intended for the lost sheep of the house of Israel and out of His unswerving obedience to the Divine will He confined His activities within those limits. Yet occasionally a Gentile crossed His path. In particular we are told of a Roman centurion requesting His help for a servant in terrible distress. In the ensuing dialogue this Gentile soldier evinces such remarkable faith and imagination as to win the unqualified approval of Jesus. And he proceeds to draw out from the incident a still wider implication: "I tell you, many will come from east and west and sit at table with Abraham, Isaac and Jacob in the kingdom of heaven, while the sons of the kingdom will be thrown into the outer darkness" (Matt. 8. 11-12. R.S.V.). Here already we are approaching St. Paul's great affirmation that in Christ Jesus there is neither Jew nor Gentile, bond nor free, for all have become sons of God through faith, all have become heirs to the promise made to the offspring of Abraham.

It is natural that St. Paul, who had grown up in the context of Rabbinic schools where the problems of man's relation to God were discussed formally and theologically, should have dealt with the question of Jew and Gentile in the purpose of God quite explicitly. Sooner or later he was bound to encounter criticism as he tried to make known the gospel of Christ in the Gentile world. Were there not privileges which belonged to the Jew only? Was it not necessary for Gentiles to be circumcised and incorporated into Judaism before they could be assured of the full blessings of the Gospel? St. Paul did not find it easy to deny the privileged position of the Hebrew people and yet in the final issue he could not allow that those who had put their faith in Christ lacked anything of the fulness of the blessings of the family of God.

The key passage may be found in the Epistle to the Galatians. St. Paul had no need to prove that the Gentiles were alienated from God, without any right to be regarded as His sons. But what of the Jews? He admits that they were children of Abraham by fleshly descent and that the Divine promises had been made to Abraham. But in so far as the Jews had been held within the system of the Law, and in so far as they had subjected themselves to the control of impersonal forces in the universe, they had failed to enjoy the freedom of children within the family of God. In other words, his claim is that while Gentiles worshipping idols had never known the joy of a personal relation to a heavenly Father, Jews who might have known it, if they had continued in the faith of their forefather Abraham, had in point of fact allowed themselves to be imprisoned within a system of law and ritual which prevented them from experiencing any freedom of access to their true Father.

Into the midst of this total situation, St. Paul says, God sent forth *His Son*. He was born of a woman, a man amongst men, subject to human limitations and temptations and yet essentially related to God as son. He was born under the Law and subject therefore to the restraints and disciplines of the Law and yet still essentially related to God as son. He came as son and lived continuously as son in spite of every inducement to sink back into the common condition as alien or servant. He maintained His filial trust even through the agonies of rejection and crucifixion and thereby inaugurated a new humanity. To all men now, whether Gentile or Jew, the way is open to become identified with the Son in faith (Gal. 2. 20) and to live as sons within the family of God. The very act of baptism means the renunciation of the old masters—idols, the Law, the impersonal powers of fate in the universe—and the putting on of Christ Himself (Gal. 3. 27). And this is not simply a change of status. The new character of sonship becomes immediately manifest as those who have been baptized into the new humanity cry "Abba Father" and show that the Spirit of the Son is already working in their hearts (Gal. 4. 6).

This whole doctrine of sonship grows out of a living situation and it is dangerous to imprison it in too formal terms. But at least we may say that according to St. Paul's teaching all men apart from Christ are enclosed in a framework of existence which prevents them from enjoying the glorious liberty of the children of God. For some the framework is that of ultimate allegiance to an idol of the imagination: for some it is that of obedience to an impersonal system of law. And because all human existence within such frameworks falls short of the glory of God, it was God's good pleasure, when the time was ripe, to send forth His Son, clothed in human flesh, living in human society, yet all the time preserving His integrity as a Son in relation to the Father. As a result of this supreme revelation, sealed by the Son into human hearts, the new family has come into being, the Church in which all are one in Christ Jesus. In these vivid terms St. Paul has confessed his own faith in God, Father, Son and Holy Spirit and shown how it can be applied universally to man in his need for a final identity and security within a more-than-human family relationship.

v

The family imagery which St. Paul employs so effectively

when writing to converts who were being assailed about the validity of their status as sons of God (did they not need to be circumcised and to become sons of Abraham if they were to be assured of a Divine inheritance?) is used with equal effectiveness by the writer of the Epistle to the Hebrews in a quite different connection. In this case the question at issue was that of priestly mediation. In Israel one family, the sons of Levi, had been appointed to act as priests on behalf of the people of God. What then was the position of Christians who had been excluded from the institutional life of Israel and seemed to have neither priest nor altar nor sacrifice? It is the purpose of the writer through his Epistle to bring words of firm assurance to those who were in doubt and uncertainty about their right of access to God and to do this by portraying Jesus as the perfect High Priest Who had brought into existence a new family of priests (comparable to the tribe of Levi), all of whom could draw near with confidence to the throne of grace.

The Epistle begins with a majestic exposition of the Divine Sonship of the One who had for a little while only been made lower than the angels. This temporary subjection had been allowed by God in order that He, Jesus, might be identified in all respects with those whom He purposed to serve. He came amongst them as a brother (Heb. 2. 11-12) sharing their flesh and blood, enduring their temptations and sufferings, and even tasting death on their behalf. All through this section the emphasis is upon the weakness, the ignorance and the waywardness of mankind. Men are sinners and their sins need to be expiated. But their sin lies primarily in their failure to draw near to God and to live as His faithful sons. They drift away from God, they fail to trust Him, they easily retreat before opposition, they quail in face of suffering, they become fearful in face of death. These are the all too obvious facts about human nature and yet the Son of God did not despise men in their weakness or refuse to be identified with them in their faithlessness. Instead He acted in all ways as their brother, their priest, their saviour, and thereby brought "many sons to glory" (Heb. 2. 10).

But such a priesthood was no sinecure. It involved the necessity of being tested at every point of human weakness, of enduring every form of human suffering, of offering his body willingly to be sacrificed, of undergoing the agony of Gethsemane and thereby carrying obedience to the very limit, of passing finally through the conflict and bitter experience of death. All this He endured as a Son on behalf of His brethren and having thus been made perfect He became the source of eternal salvation to all who obey Him (Heb. 5. 9). Nowhere in the New Testament are the implications of a true family relationship more movingly displayed. He comes among men as their brother in order that He may draw them back into the family of God. He acts as priest for the family in order that through Him the other members may be sanctified and may in turn become priests on behalf of the wider family. He, the Son, Who has gathered into the realm of divinity a total human experience (apart from sin), now stands ministering in the heavenly temple and is able to save to the uttermost all who draw near to God through Him.

It would be quite unfair to the purpose of the writer of this Epistle to attempt to deduce from his exhortation any strict dogmatic theses or formulations. His concern is to stir the imagination of those to whom he writes. He depicts the glory of the Son—one who is the beginning and end of the created order, the reflection in humanity of the Divine nature, the source from which the whole universe is sustained. He then takes for granted the whole priestly framework of the Old Testament—the priesthood, the temple, the sacrifices—and sets the work of the Divine Son firmly within this context. He is High Priest within a new family of priests. He has offered the comprehensive sacrifice through His all-embracing death. He is minister within a new sanctuary and according to the provisions of a new covenant. All the time it is as Son that He performs this priestly office and now it is for His brethren to become identified with Him and to offer through Him the sacrifice of praise and thanksgiving continually. The riddle of how the Divine could become human, how the deathless could taste death, how the eternal priesthood could be exercised in time, is not solved. But the Divine-human nature of the Son of God is affirmed and the possibility of the weak, erring brother becoming a responsible member of the family of God is unhesitatingly affirmed. To draw near with faith to the Father, to accept with patience the discipline of sons and to remember with compassion the needs of the brethren —these are the marks of those who have responded to the heavenly call and are proving faithful members of the Divine household.

VI

In the first three Gospels the Divine Sonship of Jesus is mentioned comparatively rarely and is never expounded systematically. Jesus reveals God as Father, dwells upon the wonder of His generosity and forgivingness and calls upon men to discover their true identity by turning to God, by accepting His forgiveness and by exercising a similar spirit of forgivingness to their neighbours. In the Epistles of St. Paul the Divine Sonship is constantly affirmed and the implications of the fact that God did not spare His Son but gave Him up freely for us all are drawn out in a spirit of amazement and profound thanksgiving. It is for man to renounce all reliance upon such false supports as race, legal righteousness, and ritual conformity and to cast himself in faith upon the Son of God. So will he discover his own true sonship and enjoy a new confidence within the family of God. In the Epistle to the Hebrews the author, having begun with an adoring recognition of the supreme revelation which God has given through His Son, goes on to show how this has made it possible for weak and sinful men to be restored to their true dignity as sons and to take their part as priests within the Divine Family. Other imagery as we shall see is also employed in these writings though the Father-Son-family of God relationships have already given us important doctrinal insights. When we come to the Johannine writings however we find a comprehensive interpretation of the coming of Jesus and of the Spirit expressed dominantly if not exclusively in terms of sonship and of the spirit of love. Here more than anywhere else in Christian literature we see the essential faith in God, Father, Son and Holy Spirit illustrated, interpreted, expanded through imagery derived from human family relationships.

As we try to understand the doctrinal implications of this presentation let us first examine the cultural background of those to whom these writings were addressed. In the case of the Synoptic Gospels and St. Paul the background is Hebraic rather than Hellenistic and the family imagery is used without reference to such matters as procreation, transmission of substance or physical survival. It is concerned above all with relationships—adoption, protection, discipline, forgiveness, granting an inheritance. It is true that man is not a disembodied spirit and that these relationships must affect his bodily welfare. But there is little reference to the father as begetter or to the son's sharing of the father's nature or to the way in which parent and child participate in a common life. These aspects of family relationship figured far more in the interests and traditions of the peoples of the Mediterranean world, not least among the Greeks, and it is against this kind of background that the Johannine writings must be set. Relationship is still of paramount importance but the physical and sacramental expressions of relationship are more prominent than in the other writings of the New Testament.

Let us now look at the Son as he is depicted in the Fourth Gospel. We see Him, during his incarnate life, utterly dependent upon God the Father. In all parts of the Gospel He is represented as having been 'sent'. He has come into the world to perform a specific mission. He comes in the name of the Father to bear witness to ultimate truth or reality. He does nothing of Himself. He is always eager to please the Father, to do the will of the Father, to finish the Father's work. This being the case, He has the right to exercise the authority of the Father in judgment and in determining the destinies of men. He, working with the Father, can give life to men: He too, in dependence upon the Father, can pronounce sentence of judgment upon those who continue in their sin. He is, in fact, the plenipotentiary of the Father, sent into the world to perform a particular mission, due to leave the world and return to the Father when the mission has been fulfilled.

All this leaves us in no doubt that in His eternal being the Son shares the glory of the Father and belongs as of right to that order of things which is described as 'above'. He is not of this world. He has come into the world but will leave the world and return to His true sphere, the 'above'. How exactly He came into the world is not defined. He became flesh and dwelt amongst men and they beheld His transcendent glory. But so far as the world in general knew He had come into existence in the same way as any other man. He was the son of Joseph from Nazareth (1. 45). He had a mother and brothers. He hungered and thirsted and sat wearily at a well-side. He rejoiced with men and shared their sorrows. Yet all the time He was the unique son and representative of the Father, moving amongst those who knew him not and bringing them to the crisis of expanding light or of deepening gloom.

If we proceed to enquire about the nature of the mission that the Son had come to fulfil, we are left in no doubt about the answer. He came into the world in order that men might not perish but might have eternal life. This is man's deepest need. By virtue of his natural inheritance he possesses life of a kind but it is always under threat of death. His natural inheritance gives him membership within an earthly family—Jew, Samaritan, Roman—and he may share its traditions and its hopes. But this is not membership of the family of God. In the natural order man may have knowledge of the world and of history and of the organization of social life. But this is not knowledge of God. *Eternal life is the life of sonship in the family of God.* Here distinctions of race no longer have significance, physical dangers and the death of the body have no final power to hurt, earthly knowledge bears no comparison with the knowledge of the Father given through His Son Jesus Christ.

But what if men fail to recognize the Son as the messenger of the Father and refuse to open the heart to receive Him as the revelation of God? This, says the writer, is the sin of the world. Numerous symbols are employed to illustrate this grim possibility. Light has come into the world and men have loved darkness rather than light. The life has been manifested and men have refused to receive it. Love has been shown through the whole mission of the Son and yet men have continued to hate. The truth has been spoken and men have preferred a lie. Sin blinds, deafens, hardens, petrifies and the end of sin is death. Yet the Son of God has come, unveiling the glory, explaining the purpose, demonstrating the nature of the Father. "And to as many as receive him and believe his words to them he has given the right to become children of God. They are born not of blood nor of the will of the flesh nor of the will of man but of God" (1. 12, 13).

This birth into the family of God is celebrated in lyrical terms in the First Epistle. Admission into the family of God is the ultimate pledge of the Father's love. Those who have been so admitted have passed from death to life, from ignorance to knowledge, from alienation to fellowship. They dwell in love towards God and towards one another, always dependent upon the perfect Son through whose

62

sacrifice they have been brought into their present state. Though they have no exact knowledge of the future they are confident that they will grow more and more into the likeness of the Son and that they will finally see Him as He is. The Eternal life into which Christians have been re-born, is the eternal relation of the Father and the Son. This relation has been manifested in an altogether unique way through the total earthly career of Jesus. Now all who respond to this manifestation in active trust and become united with Him in a living relationship enter into the possession of eternal life for they are related to the Father in virtue of their new-found relationship with the Son.

VII

It remains to speak of the Spirit in the imagery of family-relationships. The title given by St. Paul is the key to the whole conception: God sent the Spirit *of His Son* into our hearts. We did not receive the spirit of slavery but we received the spirit of sonship. When we cry "Abba Father" it is the Spirit himself bearing witness with our spirit that we are the children of God. Whatever difficulties may be involved in regard to the personal status of the Spirit, the general picture could hardly be clearer. In the eternal relation of Father and Son the uniting bond is *a spirit* which, being unique and eternal, can only be known as *The Spirit*. Between an earthly father and his son there exists ideally a spirit of mutual trust, mutual demand, mutual restraint, mutual help which we try to summarize in the one word love. This spirit of love does not exist in a vacuum or in a theoretical formula: it only exists within the active inter-relationship of the two parties concerned, though indeed it has the mysterious capacity of reproducing itself within the active inter-relationship of other parties also. We therefore refer concretely to this spirit as manifested in ordinary human life as a spirit of love and when we try to speak of the eternal relationship in heaven we can only speak similarly of The Spirit of Love. The Spirit of Love has, it is true, no independent existence. But as we try to speak of this Spirit operating between the Father and the Son it is hard to see how we can speak of such a spirit in other than *personal* terms.

As is well-known, St. Paul often comes very near to identifying the Spirit and the Son. He speaks of Christ and the Spirit almost interchangeably and refers without hesitation to the Spirit of Christ. This is not in the least unnatural when we remember how easy it is to identify a man with the quality of the attitudes and activities which characterize his daily life. Yet while every person has an ultimate distinctive identity, the qualities of the links between persons are not of infinite variety. We are bound to classify these bonds under such general terms as hate, fear, apprehension, sacrifice, care, integrity. An individual is never totally identified with any of these 'spirits' in his relationships with others. But the Spirit, active in the relationship between the Father and the Son is in fact an eternal Spirit, the Spirit with which the Father is totally identified, the Spirit with which the Son is totally identified. We can only speak of the Spirit in symbols or in words used to describe human relationships. And it is not surprising that St. Paul, in his own employment of such symbols, sometimes comes near to identifying the Son, Who had showed the qualities of relationship expressive of the Spirit so vividly in His own earthly life, with the Spirit Who is Himself the source and expression of those qualities.

Yet when we try in some measure to formalize the doctrine we are bound to say that whereas Jesus, in the days of His flesh, was constantly relating Himself to others in the spirit of love, joy, peace, patience, kindness, goodness, faithfulness, gentleness, self-control (Gal. 5. 22. R.S.V.) and that therefore, when He was amongst men, it was this spirit that was constantly being manifested: yet in formal terms we affirm that it is the Holy Spirit Who is eternally the Spirit of love, the Spirit of joy, the Spirit of peace etc. And similarly whereas Jesus Himself, in His earthly life, perfectly evinced the spirit of sonship towards God and brotherhood towards His fellow men yet in more formal terms it is the Holy Spirit Who is eternally the Spirit of Sonship, the Spirit of brotherhood, the Spirit of Love. The person of the Christ is so associated with actions and attitudes of love that St. Paul can pray for other members of the Father's family that Christ may dwell in their hearts by faith. Yet, as the full context of the passage shows, the indwelling power is more formally defined as the Spirit and it is through the activity of the Spirit that the whole family becomes bound together in the mutual relationship of Love.

As we have already seen the theme of eternal life is dominant in the Johannine writings and part of the author's concern is to show how that eternal life may be received and experienced in the here and now. To make this clear he draws upon the teaching of the Lord in which symbols from the wider life of the home and its surroundings were used to

65

reveal the processes of the life of the Spirit. The vine growing in the courtyard, for example, is the symbol of the body of believers who abide in the Son and He in them through the Spirit. The shepherd gathers his own into the sheepfold and lays down his life for the sheep. He is so identified with them that the inter-relationship is comparable to that between Himself and the Father in the Spirit. The Son gives new wine to the wedding guests, offers living water to the woman at the well, provides bread for the multitude, brings light to the man born blind, restores His friend Lazarus to life—in all these ways He mediates the Spirit. It is not the symbol in itself that is of profit—"the flesh profiteth nothing"—but the Spirit Who takes the symbol and uses it to convey the life of God to the believing soul. Water, breath, words, bread were all used by the Son of Man as a medium through which He could communicate the life of the Spirit to men.

In the precise context of the imagery of the family, the doctrine of the Church and Ministry and Sacraments remains intimate and informal. The all-important conception is that of absolute freedom of intercourse between the Father and the Son and its extension to all who come to the Father through the Son. This intercourse is realized supremely in and through the life of prayer: the Son engages in constant conversation with the Father and encourages believers to ask and receive that their joy may be full. Those who believe on the name of the Son of God are incorporated into the Family of God (the Church), they are placed under the guardianship of faithful shepherds (the Ministry) and they are regenerated and ever renewed through the use of symbolic media—water, bread, wine, breath (the Sacraments). This is not formalized doctrine. It is a vivid image of the fulness of life within the Family of God. In the eternal order the Father and the Son enjoy an unbroken relationship in and through the Spirit of Love. In the temporal order the Son of Man by His life and death and resurrection expresses this same spirit of love and draws into the enjoyment of eternal life all who receive His revelation and believe on His name.

Chapter Four

THE REDEEMED SOCIETY

THE family, the home, the land—these are man's dearest possessions. Whatever form the family may take, however simple the home may be, in whatever country the land may be situated, nothing can take the place of these fundamental institutions. A life which has been deprived of these supports at its beginning will forever lack roots. A life which has not only begun with these advantages but has also stretched out beyond them to enjoy the experience of love within a divine family, the security of an eternal home and the possession of a heavenly inheritance, is like a tree planted by the water-side that sends out its roots and does not fear when the heat comes. Rooted and grounded in love, such a life can grow up into all the fulness of God.

I

Yet one of the strangest things in the history of mankind is the unwillingness of those who are secure and well-established to remain forever content with their lot. The growing child wants to explore the territory outside the bounds of security: the adolescent wants to leave the comfort of the home and to risk the dangers of the frontier: the adventurer wants to climb mountains and descend into the depths of the ocean and to pioneer into outer space. Out of these so varied situations have come a vast collection of images. Innumerable myths have been constructed telling of the exploits of heroes, the loyalty of followers, the dangers encountered, the difficulties overcome, the victories achieved. The factors involved are more complex than those associated with home and family. There is often a conflict of loyalties, a sense of guilt linked with the sense of emancipation. The achievements of freedom in one direction may well lead to a more rigorous bondage in another. Freedom from irksome and cramping circumstances does not necessarily result in the enjoyment of constructive freedom in ampler surroundings. A man hailed as a physical hero may be a moral coward. Having brought freedom to many captives he may himself fall victim to the wiles of a seducer.

Just as the imagery of the life of religion draws upon that of the home and family so also it draws upon that of the hero and the struggle for freedom. A certain dualism is immediately involved because of the contrast between the security of the home and the uncertainty beyond the frontier. The most natural tendency is to identify the home with all that is pleasant, desirable, trust-worthy and life-giving, and that which is outside with all that is sinister, threatening, equivocal and death-dealing. Yet it can also happen that the child or the social-group, in the effort to break out into a new freedom, can reverse the identification and regard the very security of the home as denoting bondage and death, the very openness of the frontier as symbolizing liberty and life. Whichever way it is, the general patterns of the imagery maintain a certain consistency. On one side life, on the other side death, on one side the good, on the other side the evil, on one side servitude, on the other side freedom. And between the two there is always the figure of the hero, the pioneer, the leader, the saviour. By widely diversified means the quality of living for a favoured few becomes radically changed. To use a convenient and comprehensible term, they are saved or they experience the joy of salvation.

It is not difficult to envisage some of the struggles which have followed the adventure out into the unknown. Man quickly becomes aware of the power residing in *water*— the water of the great river or the vast ocean or the mighty flood: the hero is such a figure as the Babylonian Marduk who gains the victory over Ti'amat, the terrible goddess of the waters. Man becomes aware of the power inherent in *darkness*—the darkness of the night or of the underground cavern or of the dense forest: the hero is pre-eminently the Sun-God who bursts forth in triumph to scatter the forces of gloom. Man becomes aware of the power inherent in *winter*—the winter of the cold or of the decline of fertility: the hero is such a figure as the Egyptian Osiris who brings renewal to vegetation and as god of Spring expels the malignities of Winter. There are powers, too, exercised by the animal-creation, by storm and tempest, by drought and frost. Surrounded by these forces, man must either conquer or himself be conquered.

But in addition to the intangible forces in the natural order which threaten his existence, man finds that every attempt to extend his area of experience is liable to be resisted by personal agents in the social order either from within his own family circle (interpreting 'family' in the widest sense) or from hostile groups outside. It is true that the forces of nature have constantly been personalized and regarded as good or evil spirits, friendly towards or opposed to man's free development. But as man emerges into history, his greater concern is with the human representatives of good or evil powers. He seeks emancipation from tyranny of every kind. He engages in the struggle with those whom he regards as his enemies. Out of the totality of this human conflict in all places and at all times, with powers celestial and powers terrestrial, with enemies remote and near at hand, have come myths, sagas, legends, dramas, stories, epics all concerned with man's struggle for freedom and salvation in the widest sense of those terms.

II

Against this general background we set the imagery of the Bible itself. If we confine ourselves to the Old Testament, the imagery of salvation is perhaps more prominent than any other symbolic pattern. The Book of Genesis introduces us in an altogether appealing way to the pastoral and family life of the Hebrew people. We read of family-relationships and customs, we watch the recurring patterns of succeeding generations, we obtain brief glimpses of other tribes and nations. The quiet tenor of the life of God's chosen family, the family of Abraham, is not seriously disturbed until towards the end of the book. Then a man Joseph appears, clearly set in a different mould from that of his brothers, leading them ultimately into strange new conditions where they were to become aliens in a foreign land. The pattern of family conformity is in process of being broken. Individuals and the tribe are moving out into new ways.

The very title Exodus suggests the character of the new Israel. From now onwards the Hebrews were destined to be a struggling and freedom-seeking people, often oppressed, often frustrated, but always hoping for the great deliverance which would usher in a new era of life and liberty. All this was viewed however not from a purely human standpoint but as part of the very purpose of God Himself. Had they been left to themselves they might have stayed for ever in Egypt. Though some found conditions exceedingly irksome, others, it would appear, were not averse to enjoying the amenities of civilization. But there was a creative individual who was destined to become a heroic leader. In the language of later times he was a man of God, a prophet, and to him it was granted to see God in a new way and to receive a new revelation of His purpose. So he returned to Egypt to summon his people to new adventure and to stir their hearts with the prospect of being able to serve the God of their fathers in freedom under His constant protection.

The remarkable events which led to the escape of a large body of slaves from Egypt and to their safe passage through the Red Sea were built up into an epic story which remained through successive centuries the constitutive image for the social and religious life of Israel. In this new revelation, God appears as the One Who is always concerned for the oppressed and afflicted and Who initiates plans for their deliverance. He controls the total situation, He acts in mysterious and wonderful ways to steer the course of history forward to its destined goal. But although He is the initiator of every act of deliverance and the transcendent controller of the total strategy of salvation, He does not disdain to use men as His deputies to identify themselves in person with suffering peoples and to lead them out towards a promised land. In the midst of the story of deliverance from Egypt there stands the towering figure of Moses who chose to share ill-treatment with the people of God rather than to enjoy the honours and pleasures of the imperial civilization. He endured as seeing Him who is invisible and was not afraid of the power of the tyrant. Moses the servant of God took his place alongside the people in their sin. He was a human symbol of the power of God coming near to deliver and to save.

There is one other striking feature of the Exodus story. On the eve of the great deliverance the people united with one another in a single cultic act of deep significance. Each household killed a lamb, applied its blood to specified parts of the home, confessed through a liturgical form the meaning of the ritual and ate the roasted flesh after preparing to leave at any moment for the journey. By this means the whole company of Israel expressed their faith in the purpose of God and received His sustaining power into their lives. In dramatic fashion the people of God identified themselves with their leader and through him with God their great Redeemer: at the same time they received their consecration to service and their empowering for the pilgrim way. In this drama of the Passover there is at least a prefiguring of the entrance of God's Spirit into the inner structure of human lives to empower and to sanctify. At the same time a powerful form is provided by which, year by year, the great deliverance can be commemorated and its benefits experienced afresh.

The threefold pattern which emerges from the Exodus story is of immense significance in the unfolding of subsequent developments in Israel's history. For a few comparatively short periods between the deliverance from Egypt and the destruction of the Temple in A.D. 70 the Jewish people enjoyed the blessings of an ordered and settled national life. Far more frequently they were struggling for their very existence against one or other of the surrounding tribes and empires. Even their relations with the powers of the natural order—plague, pestilence, drought, flood— were by no means smooth and easy. But the enemy *par excellence* was the predatory and warlike nation—the Amorites, the Philistines, the Syrians, the Babylonians, the Greeks, the Romans. Even during the wilderness pilgrimage they were open to attack. They fought their way into the promised land but then had to defend their borders against every kind of foe. Their stronghold, Jerusalem, was ultimately sacked and their leading citizens deported. Time and again they were under threat from the comings and goings of imperial forces. No wonder that the archetype of Israel's history was a situation in which the very survival of the nation was at stake and in which the mighty deliverance of God, mediated through a hero-prophet and experienced through a renewed act of faith, became a miraculous reality.

In some ways, to be sure, this led to what can only be regarded as a crude portrayal of God as the Lord of Hosts, the Lord mighty in battle, the Captain of salvation who initiates a campaign, develops its strategy and carries it forward to a successful conclusion.

Let God arise, let his enemies be scattered;
Let those who hate him flee before him!
The Lord gives the command;
    great is the host of those who bore the tidings:
"The kings of the armies, they flee, they flee."
The women at home divide the spoil
                        (Ps. 68. 1, 11, 12. R.S.V.).

Come, behold the works of the Lord,
    how he has wrought desolations in the earth.
He makes wars cease to the end of the earth;
He breaks the bow, and shatters the spear,
He burns the chariots with fire! (Ps. 46. 8, 9. R.S.V.)

Prophet and psalmist did not hesitate to use the imagery of the battlefield and of the clashes of warlike peoples in order to exalt the name of the supreme controller of the conflict, the One Who redeems His people from distress and threat of destruction and leads them forward to the attainment of salvation and peace.

Similarly the leaders, the judges and the prophets of Israel were often cruel and ruthless. Joshua, commissioned to continue the work of Moses, does not hesitate to burn the city of Ai and destroy all its inhabitants. Samson, empowered we are told by the Spirit of the Lord, slew a thousand of the Philistines by his own hand. Elijah, encouraged by his vindication at Carmel, gives orders that the four hundred prophets of Baal shall be seized and ruthlessly destroyed at the brook Kishon. Nahum pronounces doom upon Nineveh in terms of a terribly realistic imagery. These are by no means isolated examples and their implications can hardly be avoided. The typical prophet-hero of Israel was fearless himself and constantly succeeded in renewing the faith and courage of his own people. He bore witness unceasingly to God as the strong deliverer of His people. He believed that however dark present circumstances might be it was the intention of the mighty Lord of hosts to preserve His people from extinction and to redeem them from the hands of their enemies. But all this was at the cost of a terribly sharp distinction between good and evil, between election and rejection, between pure worship and idolatry, between keeping the law and being accursed. To declare the mighty acts of deliverance of God, the Lord of Hosts, almost inevitably had as its corollary the declaration of the terrible acts of destruction upon the enemies of His people.

Finally the redeemed people themselves, having been preserved through a time of distress and great anxiety and having been brought to a new experience of freedom and expansion, tended not unnaturally to blacken the past and the wickedness of their tormentors and to glorify the present and the marks of the Divine favour which they now enjoyed. Redemption easily came to be viewed in terms of absolute separation. A major ingredient of new freedom was an uncompromising hatred of former oppressors. So the ritual ceremonies which sanctified the corporate life of Israel came easily to be interpreted as marks of strict separation from the evil practices of unbelievers and as opportunities for an almost fanatical rededication to the God Who was able to judge and destroy their enemies. The spirit which animated the people of God was less a spirit of power struggling for the attainment of wider justice than a spirit of moral superiority seeking to establish a separate kingdom of the saints.

All this must be allowed and the varying excesses and distortions must be fully recognized. Yet the overall pattern of myth and ritual, story and sacrament, remains entirely valid and of profound importance as a receptacle for the coming revelation in Christ Himself. What then may be singled out as the positive and abiding elements in this imagery, elements ready to be taken up and used in later Christian confessions of faith?

In the first place there is the magnificent new stress on the fact that God is the Saviour and Deliverer of the weak and the oppressed. Whether it be a child seeking to struggle forwards to its own identity and selfhood, whether it be a tribe or nation striving to escape from the bonds of paternalism or colonialism into a new independence, whether it be an oppressed section of the community writhing in its agony and crying out for redemption, the positive assurance of the Old Testament is that God cares for all such and that God will save. The noble words of Exodus 3. 7-8 are definitive for every comparable situation:

I have seen the affliction of my people
I have heard their cry:
I know their sufferings:
I have come down to deliver.

However perversely these words may be misinterpreted or misapplied, they constitute a focal image of the character of God and their basic implications are not rescinded by the later Christian revelation.

In the second place there is the demonstration through

the careers of the long succession of heroes of faith that God Who initiates the great act of deliverance fulfils it, on the plane of history, through the agency of a trusted representative man. How such men arise out of the ordinariness of human existence and tower above their contemporaries is a mystery never explained except in terms of God's choosing. But their significance is paramount. Their entry upon the human scene is usually quiet in the extreme. At an early stage they begin to be stirred by the needs of their compatriots and by the purpose of salvation which they are sure God intends on behalf of the distressed. This stirring leads almost inevitably to conflict: to a struggle with a man's own diffidence, with the complacency of his fellows, with the opposition of vested interests, with the contempt of those in authority. The conflict comes to its crisis and the servant of the Lord may often seem to have been crushed by reactionary powers. But because the ultimate Redeemer and Deliverer is God Himself, the work of the human saviour is not in vain. He *is* human and he displays human weaknesses but at best he pioneers the way into a new freedom and saves His people out of the hands of their enemies. The focal image of the Lord's Servant who is the Saviour-Hero is given vivid expression in Isaiah 53 and again its basic implications retain their validity within the fulness of the Christian revelation.

Thirdly there is the emphasis, renewed again and again, that what the Hero-Saviour makes possible must be appropriated by the community through a solemn act of participation. As I have shown, the Exodus was celebrated by the observance of Passover in which all who were ready to go out on the adventure into freedom first separated themselves by the blood of the sacrifice and then shared in the common food. But Passover was to be an annual feast and in point of fact it retained its place more firmly than any other ceremony within the yearly cycle of tribal observance. At Passover the people of God made a solemn memorial, not merely remembering deliverance as an event of the past but re-experiencing salvation in the circumstances of the present, and looking forward to their final redemption in the future. In this sacramental drama there was a real communion of spirits and a renewal of the sense of freedom which had been realized in the first instance under the leadership of Moses. Special scriptures were read, special psalms were sung, a definite liturgy was enacted and in and through all the Spirit of power came again into the hearts of men, enabling them to recover strength for the pilgrim journey and hope of the final goal. The memorial of redemption provides a focal image of the work of the Spirit in the inner life of the community, an image which does not grow outmoded before the era of the fuller revelation in Christ.

Before coming to the New Testament proclamation of the Messiah we encounter the remarkable messages of the great prophets of the Exile—Jeremiah, Ezekiel and the Second Isaiah. In spite of what appeared to have been unmitigated disaster, these men still looked forward with hope to a deliverance which would be much more than a redemption from a foreign yoke and a restoration to the land of their fathers. They did not hesitate to associate the calamity and distress which had befallen their people with the low standards of moral and religious life which had been all too characteristic of pre-exilic times. So in proclaiming the certainty of a new deliverance they insisted that this would

be not simply an emancipation from the enforced subjuga-
tion of a foreign power but rather a release from injustice and
lawlessness within the community of Israel itself. In their
view the time of exile was to be regarded as a period of
punishment and discipline and refining. When this process
had gone far enough God would intervene, would bring
judgment upon Israel's tormentors and would bring His
people to a new order of experience in which they would be
"saved by the Lord with everlasting salvation". Sometimes
in these prophecies the figure of a Messiah appears dimly
and the outpouring of a new Spirit is foreseen. But the
greatest emphasis of all is upon what God Himself will do
for His people by the might of His own outstretched arm.
The power of the oppressor seemed so strong that it was
hard to think of a new Moses or a new Joshua being able to
break out into freedom. In so far as a leader was envisaged at
all, he came to be thought of more as a superhuman figure
to be sent miraculously from above as the agent of God's
redemption.

v

The events with which the New Testament is primarily
concerned were, to say the least, startling and the interpretation of the events was nothing less than revolutionary.
In the earliest Christian preaching the apostolic witnesses
affirmed that a man Jesus of Nazareth, who had during his
lifetime relieved many of their physical ills and distresses,
had ultimately been seized by the Jewish authorities and put
to death. But God had raised Him from the dead and now He
was continuing His saving work through the Spirit Who had

come with power amongst men. In the light of all that had happened, in spite of an initial bewilderment concerning the trial and crucifixion of Jesus, they did not hesitate to proclaim that He was indeed the looked-for Messiah, the Saviour of Israel. Henceforth there could be salvation in none other for there was no other name under heaven given amongst men by which they could be saved (Acts. 4. 12).

In course of time other events leading up to and resulting from the Crucifixion were added to the central core of witness but at the beginning attention was focussed on the double-sided event of Jesus' Death and Resurrection. The wonder of the deliverance from death and Hades never ceased to amaze and inspire the early Christians but at the same time the unexpectedness of the suffering and death continued to puzzle them. The splendour of the first confirmed their claim that Jesus was the promised Messiah: the shame of the second made it almost impossible to persuade their fellow-countrymen that this claim could be true. Some way must be found of holding together these two antithetical positions if the Christian gospel was not to be dismissed as sheer absurdity. And the way which they took —a way already pioneered by the great prophets of the Exile—was that of relating the sin of the community to the suffering and even the death of the saviour. It was because of sin that suffering and death had to be endured. It was through resurrection that the grip of sin had been broken. If the Jews in the time of Jesus had been sinless in their corporate and individual lives and if their servitude had been simply due to the oppression of a tyrannical Roman overlord, then the death of the one who essayed to be their Saviour would have seemed a final refutation of His ability to act on their behalf. If on the other hand His identification with a sinful people led inevitably to the sharing of their judgment, even when that judgment was inflicted by an alien power, then judgment having been borne it was possible to see in the Resurrection God's vindication of the saving act and the opening of the kingdom of heaven to all believers.

With this general introduction we are now in a position to look in more detail at the New Testament confession of faith in God, Father, Son and Holy Spirit in terms of our second pattern of imagery. The confession can now best be defined as that of faith in God, Redeemer, Messiah and Holy Spirit of Power. To choose the most appropriate title for God the Transcendent, Who delivers man out of his misery and distress and failure and despair, is not easy. The Old Testament speaks of deliverance, redemption, salvation. Of these three, redemption is perhaps the most appropriate to apply to the deliverance from Egypt and it is this event which establishes the pattern of God's saving activity for subsequent Hebrew history. So we may speak of God as Transcendent Redeemer. The prophetic figures of the Old Testament, the heroes, the champions, the pioneers, gradually flow towards one all-inclusive figure, the Messiah. He is to lead God's people in the final struggle out of bondage into freedom, out of death into life. So we may speak of God with us, God at our side, as the Messiah, the Christ. And when this Messiah has been exalted and has poured forth His Spirit into the community, this Spirit who is ever working towards release, expansion, and freedom, is the Spirit of *Dynamis*, the Holy Spirit of indwelling power. So we may speak of the God Who is in us as the Spirit of Power. We confess Him Who is Redeemer, Messiah, Holy

82

Spirit of Power and we proceed now to see how this confession is substantiated in the New Testament as a whole.

VI

At the beginning of St. Luke's Gospel we find two very significant cultic hymns commonly known as the Magnificat and the Benedictus. These provide an invaluable insight into the atmosphere of simple Jewish piety at the beginning of the Christian era and show how prominent was the conception of God as Saviour and Redeemer of the oppressed.

> He has shown strength with his arm,
> He has scattered the proud in the imagination of their hearts,
> He has put down the mighty from their thrones,
> And exalted those of low degree (R.S.V.) (1. 51-52).
> He has turned to his people, saved them and set them free,
> And has raised up a deliverer of victorious power from the
>   house of his servant David.
> Age after age he proclaimed by the lips of his holy prophets,
> That he would deliver us from our enemies, out of the hands
>   of all who hate us (1. 68-71. N.E.B.).

Whatever might be the ideas and practices of the religious leaders, the common people continued to hope for some new intervention of God in which He would relieve their poverty, heal their sicknesses, deliver them from the power of evil spirits, and guide their feet into the way of peace.

According to the later writers of the New Testament, this had indeed been the age-long purpose of God. It is the will of God our Saviour that all men should find salvation and come to know the truth (1 Tim. 2. 4). The grace of God our Saviour has dawned upon the world to bring

83

healing for all mankind (Titus 2. 11). Whether it be physical ills or moral ills, whether it be oppression from without or bondage from within, whatever hinders man from the free expansion of his personality towards its true goal is contrary to the will of God. God wills salvation: God is always directing His activity towards salvation. This is an essential part of the message of the New Testament and the supreme pledge of this truth is the coming of the Messiah to be the effective agent of God's saving work.

Each of the Lucan hymns already quoted, having confessed that the saving activity of God continues from generation to generation, focuses its attention upon the particular act by which a maiden has been chosen to be the mother of the Messiah, a forerunner has been appointed to prepare the way for the bringer of salvation. The writers of the Pastorals who acknowledge God as Saviour go on to speak of the mediator Christ Jesus, Himself man, Who sacrificed Himself to win freedom for all mankind, to set us free from all wickedness and to make us a pure people marked out for His own. In Christ, says the author of the Epistle to the Ephesians, God chose us before the world was founded: in Christ our release is secured and our sins are forgiven through the shedding of His blood. And in the definitive pronouncement at the beginning of St. Matthew's Gospel the infant Messiah is given the name Jesus, a name denoting Saviour, for He will save his people from their sins. The Messiah is sent to effect salvation: He is always seeking to save that which is lost. This is the second abiding theme of the New Testament.

Thirdly, the Spirit brings to effective realization that which has been made possible by the Messiah in His saving work. At an earlier point in this chapter I suggested that the noble words of Exodus 3. 7-8 provide us with a focal image of the character of God in His saving work. A comparable image, equally definitive for the incarnate work of the Son is to be found in St. Luke 4. 18-19. Having received the assurance of His vocation at the Jordan and having passed through the supreme testing of the wilderness—temptation, Jesus comes in the full power of the Spirit into Galilee. Then in the Nazareth synagogue he gives the classic definition of His mission:

> The Spirit of the Lord is upon me,
> He has anointed me to preach good news to the poor.
> He has sent me to proclaim release to the captives
>> and recovering of sight to the blind,
>> to set at liberty those who are oppressed,
>> to proclaim the acceptable year of the Lord (R.S.V.).

This was the Spirit revealed in all Jesus' activities. He came not to destroy men's lives but to save them. And the same Spirit, entering at length into the hearts of the apostles, enabled them to continue His saving work. Men took knowledge of them that they had been with Jesus. His healing, freedom-giving, joy-bringing activities were being reproduced and recapitulated in the men who had been empowered by the Spirit of the Messiah. This Spirit of power does not act to compel or bludgeon or dragoon: this Spirit acts rather in power to set men free, to remove the bondage of guilt, to reveal new possibilities of advance, to unite men in every way with the saving work of the Messiah. The God Whom we confess and adore is the God of Salvation: Redeemer, Messiah, Holy Spirit of Power.

I have spoken of man's struggle to obtain his freedom. But so far I have said little of the struggle involved in the precise act of liberation. If God is the Saviour, if the Messiah is His agent in the saving work, what does this mean in terms of actual conflict with the forces of resistance? Does God save man by exercising an almighty fiat on his behalf? Does the Messiah tread down His enemies without harm or hurt to Himself? Even man's own judgment rebels against the acceptance of a salvation so easily gained.

> It is by no breath,
> Turn of eye, wave of hand, that salvation
>   joins issue with death!

And although Christian orthodoxy has hesitated to say without qualification that God can suffer, yet nothing is clearer from the Bible than that the image of a suffering God has a place in the total Christian revelation.

So far as the Old Testament is concerned this image appears infrequently and only indirectly. It is possible to gather references to the way in which human sin and defection brings pain to the heart of God or to the way in which the sufferings of his people are felt by God Himself. But in the main God is above the conflict, initiating, controlling, but not directly involved. It is different with His agents of redemption. Moses and the prophets, the righteous man and the faithful servant of the Lord, all become involved in the conflict with evil powers and earthly tyrannies and few escape scatheless. The prophet becomes the martyr, the servant becomes the sufferer, in the struggle for salvation.

In the New Testament everything becomes more intense and more concentrated. We soon become aware that this is the central conflict of all time. This is the crisis of the world and its rulers. The Adversary, who is the prince of this world, is receiving a mortal blow. Jesus inaugurates His mission with a symbolic conflict in the wilderness where He joins issue with the Adversary and at great personal cost wins the victory. He comes into Galilee proclaiming that the Kingdom of God has come near and implying that the powers of light are joining issue with the powers of darkness. His own works of salvation constitute an invasion of the enemy's territory. He comes to cast fire on the earth, to bring not peace but a sword. He challenges the demonic influences which hold men in thrall and goes steadily forward in His work of redemption. But the dark clouds begin to gather, the powers of evil close in around Him and the final conflict is joined. The Messiah suffers, goes to the Cross, dies. He identifies Himself not only with the living but also with the dead. And the Satanic army appears to have gained the victory.

Yet nothing is more characteristic of the new Christian era, nothing is more significant for every early Christian witness, than the Resurrection of Jesus the Messiah from the dead. He had borne the heat of the conflict. He had constantly spent Himself in the agony of prayer and at the last had so prayed that His sweat became like great drops of blood falling down to the ground. He had refused to save Himself while engaged in the mighty task of saving others. So His hands and His feet and His side, His words and His works and His prayers—all received the imprint of the conflict before they were taken up in His resurrected humanity into

87

the very being of God. He died but is alive for evermore. He the Conqueror holds the keys of Death and Hades. He set us free but at the cost of His own blood. It is the incarnate God, the Messiah, the Agent of Salvation, who bears the marks of suffering and no doctrine can claim to be Christian unless it bears full witness to this fact. Furthermore, inasmuch as it is the transcendent Redeemer of mankind Who sends forth His Messiah, anoints Him as His representative, supports Him in His activity and finally receives Him again into the sphere of eternal salvation, it is impossible to dissociate suffering and dereliction entirely from the eternal being of God Himself. We speak in mysteries. But that which we confess of the Son we confess of the Father. Confessing that the Messiah suffered and was crucified we confess also that God our Redeemer knows the awfulness of ultimate suffering in the depths of His eternal being.

But what is true of God our Redeemer and of His Messiah is also true of the Spirit of power who works in and through the community of salvation. Nothing is clearer from the Acts of the Apostles than that the continuation of the work of the Messiah is at the cost of conflict and suffering in His Church. A James and a Stephen are identified with the Christ in death: a Peter and a Paul are identified in imprisonment and torture and ultimate martyrdom: others are identified in the conflict of prayer and the agony of sin-bearing. But though it was they who laboured, yet they would have been the first to affirm that it was not they but the Spirit of the Messiah working in them. His mission of salvation must at all costs go forward. The opposition of earthly and demonic powers did not grow less. And those who held special responsibility as leaders of the messianic band were bound to be the special targets of the forces of evil. By the Holy Spirit and by the power of God they engaged in the struggle. They appeared to be deceivers and yet were true, to be unknown and yet were well known, as dying and yet were alive, as chastened and yet were not killed, as sorrowful yet were always rejoicing, as poor yet making many rich, as having nothing they yet possessed all things. All this is the life of the Spirit in the Church and particularly in the ministry. And all is of God Who is the Saviour of all men and Who has sent His Messiah to be the Saviour of the world.

VIII

So far I have made only the briefest reference to St. Paul. But it is to him that we must look for the most sustained and comprehensive doctrine of salvation in the early Church. No man of whom we have record experienced so dramatic a release from a life of servitude into a life of freedom. This truth has been admirably expressed by one of the leading modern interpreters of St. Paul's theology and I quote his statement in full:

"His experience on the road to Damascus led to a tremendous deliverance and transformation in the life of Saul of Tarsus. On the one hand it meant for him redemption from the power of sin, from the bondage of the Law and from the dominion of unseen forces of evil, what we might call the demonic element in life. The terms he uses to proclaim the same truth are familiar, justification to describe his freedom from guilt before

89

God, remission to express the cancelling of his debts to God, and reconciliation to mark the removal of his enmity towards God. These words do not refer to distinct acts or effects, they are different ways of expressing the one truth, that in Christ Paul had been freed from what had formerly frustrated him. But not only had Christ broken for him the dominance of evil, He had also supplied him with new power. The deliverance of Paul had a positive content. His Epistles are full of antitheses setting forth the difference that Christ has made. He refers to an old man who was crucified with Christ, to the new man put on through Christ; bondage has given place to liberty; life in the flesh to life in the Spirit. He had been delivered from the power of darkness and translated into the Kingdom of His dear Son; delivered from the present evil age into the new age.

Henceforth, it was Paul's primary task in life and thought to interpret this experience in terms which would be understood by his contemporaries."[1]

Let us follow this interpretation in rather more detail.

Looking first at the picture of servitude or slavery we ask who were the oppressive overlords who held the apostle in bondage? Four stand out clearly. First there was Sin, a malevolent force operating universally through man's flesh: secondly there was the Law, an ambiguous power designed for man's uplift but often bringing about his downfall: then there were the more intangible forces of the spirit world, the demons, the Elements, the superhuman forces of evil in

[1] W. D. Davies, *Paul and Rabbinic Judaism*, p. 36

the heavens (N.E.B., Ephesians 6. 12): finally there was the last enemy, Death. These four constituted as it were the prison-walls of man's existence. Or to put it more accurately, they were quasi-personal gaolers who had built the walls and were now standing on guard watching every possible way of escape.

St. Paul never falters in his assurance that the rigid control of these evil tyrannies has been broken. Man is potentially free. It is for him now to exercise this freedom and to go forward on the road to eternal salvation. But how has this great deliverance been effected? And how can man in point of fact take advantage of it? In brief the answer is that the Messiah came forth as the champion to engage these powers in mortal combat: that in each case he appeared to have been vanquished: that God raised Him from the dead and gave Him glory: and that the fruits of His victory are now available to all who toil in the human situation. It then follows that man's only requirement, if he is to share in this great salvation, is Faith: faith in the sense of a complete identification with the Messiah in His death and resurrection: faith in the sense of a deliberate putting off of every allegiance to the forces of tyranny and a putting on of a new devotion to the Messiah who loved men and gave Himself for them.

It is worth mentioning at this point that the imagery of deliverance is not the only framework employed by St. Paul. We have already seen how powerfully he uses the image of the family and later we shall be examining his references to familiar processes of law and justice. But for the moment we can imagine him with his Hebrew background, vividly aware of what the Exodus meant in his nation's history, sealed into this deliverance through his own circumcision, renewing it annually at the Passover season, looking forward to the great redemption yet to be enacted when all the enemies of God's people would be finally overcome. At the same time we can imagine him sharing the disquiet of many of his contemporaries because of the evil that was in the world and because of the fateful influence exercised by unseen demonic powers. Above all we can imagine him troubled by the conflict of forces in his own soul, the impulse towards moral excellence being harried by a sinful tendency which seemed able to frustrate all his efforts to obey the Divine commands.

St. Paul's outstanding contribution to Christian theology is his transformation of Old Testament redemption-imagery by setting at its very centre the Messiah, crucified and risen. The bondage in Egypt is replaced by the universal bondage under Sin and Death: the hero-redeemer Moses is replaced by the Messiah Who identifies Himself with mankind to the very limit of obedience, even to the death of a Cross: the triumph at the Red Sea is fulfilled in the victory of the Resurrection: the redeemed covenant-people is replaced by the people of the new covenant, those who through faith have put on Christ and been sealed by the Holy Spirit of promise: the final redemption into the promised land is replaced by the final reception into the Messianic Kingdom where Christ will be all and in all. There is no strict consistency in the use of the imagery. Sometimes the tyranny of Sin is in view, sometimes the tyranny of Death. Sometimes the Messiah is the heroic saviour, sometimes he is the willing passover victim. But the doctrinal implications are unmistakably clear. Through the death of the Messiah a way has been created for men to become dead to every form of bondage. Through His Resurrection those who have died with Him will also live with Him, sharing in the present age His Spirit of life and power, sharing in the age to come the fulness of the eternal inheritance.

As far as the individual is concerned the most extended use of this imagery is to be found in Romans chapters 5-7. There we read of the entrance of sin and death into the world as the result of Adam's transgression. The details of the Fall-story need not be pressed. The point is that the world is regarded as having been corrupted in all its parts through the defection of a primal responsible creature. The whole created order has thus been subjected to bondage. In his own heart man is torn this way and that way through conflicting desires and comes ultimately to realize that he is the slave of the totality which St. Paul calls the flesh. Unless there be some intervention from outside this closed system, there is no possibility of redemption. Man cannot help himself and the temporary structures introduced to save the world from anarchy and dissolution cannot do more than restrain—they cannot release. So we hear the bitter cry: "Miserable creature that I am, who is there to rescue me out of this body doomed to death?" (7. 24, N.E.B.). And the significant answer flashes back: "God alone, through Jesus Christ our Lord."

IX

The essential elements in the saving work of the Messiah are that He came in a form like that of man's sinful nature and that He allowed His body to be offered as a means of deliverance from sin. In other words, He became so identified with man in his slavery to sin that He could offer Himself as the price for man's remission from his slavery. The principle that a representative figure could, by offering himself, purchase freedom for others was generally accepted. Jesus came voluntarily into the situation: He was a representative and inclusive figure: His sacrifice was of infinite value: it was therefore such as to open the door into freedom for all who would identify themselves in faith with the One Who had led the way. Such a faith must mean death and resurrection for the redeemed just as it had meant death and resurrection for the Redeemer. Faith in St. Paul's teaching was never just a shallow assent, an intellectual recognition of objective fact. It was commitment of one person wholeheartedly to Another. It was identification in every possible respect. This meant that all who responded in faith to the supreme act of the Messiah in death and resurrection were *ipso facto* committed to the same pattern. This pattern would be worked out (a) Sacramentally (b) Ethically (c) Eschatologically.

a. The sacramental expression of the death-resurrection pattern was twofold. In the first place the ceremony of baptism was regarded as the transformation of the Old Testament ceremony of circumcision. The latter symbolized the cutting away of a portion of the old life and the bestowal of fresh potency for the new. Baptism symbolized the crucifixion of the old self and the destruction of the body of sin: it symbolized also the union with the risen Christ in newness of life.

Do you not know that all of us who have been baptized into Christ Jesus were baptized into His death? We were buried therefore with Him by baptism into death, so that as Christ was raised from the dead by the glory of the Father, we too might walk in newness of life (Rom. 6. 3-4, R.S.V.).

In the second place the celebration of the Lord's Supper was regarded as the transformation of the Old Testament celebration of Passover. The latter symbolized the coming forth out of Egyptian bondage and the creation of a new society in freedom and hope. The Lord's Supper symbolized the participation of the new community in the Lord's death: it symbolized also the entrance into the new covenant and participation in His risen life. In the Lord's Supper the Church repeatedly gains its identity by participating in the death and resurrection of the Messiah. Sacramentally the Church is to be defined as the company of those who have become identified with Christ in death and resurrection through baptism and who are ever being renewed in that identification through their participation in the bread and the cup of the new Passover.

b. Ethically the death-resurrection pattern was expressed in varying catechetical forms of the early Church. Egypt was the type of all sinful ways and habits: the Red Sea passage was the type of deliverance into freedom and hope. St. Paul calls for a purging out of the old leaven of malice and evil, the celebration of Christ's victory with the unleavened bread of sincerity and truth. The Epistle to the Ephesians includes a long catalogue of the characteristic marks of the old nature, all of which are to be "put off". It follows with a comparable list for the new nature, "created after the likeness of God in true righteousness and holiness", all of which are to be "put on" (4. 22-24). Perhaps most striking of all the Epistle to the Colossians pictures the ethical life of the Christian community in terms of a putting to death of all that is earthly, a setting of the mind on things above where Christ is seated at the right hand of God. "For you have died and your life is hid with Christ in God." Evil things—impurity, covetousness, malice, slander—are to be put away. The good things—compassion, kindness, lowliness, patience, forgiveness—are to be put on and above all, writes the Apostle, "put on love which binds everything together in perfect harmony" (3. 14, R.S.V.). The pattern of death and resurrection determines the ethical life of the Christian community and brings it growingly into conformity with the image of its creator.

c. Eschatologically St. Paul's whole conception is governed by the pattern of the event which has already happened, namely the death and resurrection of the Messiah. Through this death and resurrection the 'Age to Come' has already dawned. Those who had been held captives by Death can now be released. They go out from the sphere of Death into the life which is hid with Christ in God. And because He, being raised from the dead, dieth no more, neither do they. In the fine words of Dr. C. H. Dodd: "They are righteous, holy, glorious, immortal, according to the prophecies, with the righteousness, holiness, glory and immortality which are His in full reality and are theirs in the communion of His Body." Having died with Christ to sin, the world and the demonic powers, they already live with Him in the assurance of His eternal kingdom.

In the great chapter 15 of the first Epistle to the Corinthians St. Paul employs various analogies to suggest how such a thing can be. A grain of wheat which falls into the ground and dies takes to itself a new form. Celestial bodies have a different kind of structure from that of earthly bodies. He works out vivid contrasts: sown in weakness, raised in power; sown a physical body, raised a spiritual body; sown as perishable, raised as imperishable. He magnifies the power of God Who can provide a new body, who can change the dead in a moment, in the twinkling of an eye. But no analogies or illustrations can fully comprehend the mystery. The all important matter is union with the Messiah in death and resurrection. Those who have in any way experienced newness of life in Christ in the present will most certainly enjoy fulness of life in Christ in the final consummation.

Chapter Five

THE HEAVENLY CITY

In what is perhaps the most impressive list of heroes of faith to be found anywhere in literature we suddenly encounter two unexpected references to a city. The whole theme of Hebrews 11 is the frontier. Faith took men away from the settled and the sown and forced them out to the desert and the uninhabited. One of the most famous of all such pioneers was Abraham. He "obeyed the call to go out to a land destined for himself and his heirs, and left home without knowing where he was to go. By faith he settled as an alien in the land promised him, living in tents, as did Isaac and Jacob, who were heirs to the same promise. For he was looking forward to the city with firm foundations, whose architect and builder is God." And indeed, so the writer of this chapter tells us, all the heroes of Jewish history "died in faith. They were not yet in possession of the things promised, but had seen them far ahead and hailed them, and confessed themselves no more than strangers or passing travellers on earth. That is why God is not ashamed to be called their God; for He has a city ready for them" (Hebrews 11. 8-10; 13-16, N.E.B.).

I

After the frontier, the city. This is the symbolic sequence revealed in the history both of the individual and of the

98

social group. The youth who has shaken himself free from the securities of the home rejoices for a period in new discovery, in fresh adventure, in the pursuit of fortune. The predatory tribe gains temporary excitement by hunting and pillaging, ever living dangerously, rejoicing in the intimate sense of brotherhood created by the sharing of so precarious an existence. But except in cases of arrested development the desire for a city is bound to grow. Man is not content to continue for ever in a state of uncertainty, disorder or anarchy. He lacks the energy to struggle indefinitely, single-handed, against all comers. The urge to make treaties and agreements, to frame laws and constitutions, to submit issues to arbitration and government, becomes insistent. And the result of voluntary restrictions on individual liberty and commitments to social justice is *the city*. The city is the symbol of the coming together of men from divers origins and varying traditions into a willed unity in which the price of restraint has to be paid for the advantage of living unmolested in a patterned order of existence.

Yet if the frontier is a complex symbol, the city is even more ambiguous. The city can represent ordered freedom: it can also represent organized slavery. It can stand as the out-ward mark of man's growing confidence and reasonableness: it can also stand as the mark of pride and fanaticism. A man chosen to rule may establish harmony and peace among sections of the community previously antagonistic to one another: on the other hand he may by favouring one section provoke bitter hostility in another and the last state may be worse than the first. The city has made possible some of the noblest achievements and some of the foulest degradations in the history of mankind.

Religious imagery has drawn heavily upon the life of the city with its centre of government and its ordered communal responsibilities. It is well-known that in the great civilizations of the ancient world—Egypt, Babylon, China and particularly later in Rome—the Emperor was accorded a divine status. The great buildings were those which provided him with a palace while he lived and a tomb when he died. The whole pattern of life was conical or pyramidal with the emperor or governor at the highest place in the centre and with all other ranks of society established in concentric circles or squares of diminishing height around him. When, as was normally the case, he was the object of religious veneration as well as the centre of social organization his subordinates, the priest-deputies, performed religious ceremonies and mediated justice between man and man. But this dual responsibility was not easy to maintain and history shows that though it may be possible to retain the sacred character of the supreme governor, lesser officials tend to become either secular or religious, not both. Civil servants then direct the affairs of the state, priests those of the temple or its subordinate sanctuaries.

This pattern of ordered life on earth was held to depend upon and in many ways to be modelled upon the ordered regularity of the heavenly bodies. The great civilizations of antiquity had their astronomers and astrologers who provided heavenly sanctions for earthly rules. The steady movements of sun, moon and stars, the ordered sequences of seasons, fertility-cycles and river-floods, the recurrence of significant shapes such as the circle, the square and the triangle, all played an influential part in the moulding of the city-state. The emperor or king had his place at the centre and was regarded as the essential link between heaven and earth. He had his appropriate dwelling-place, also at the centre and an appropriate liturgy to perform. If all was right between heaven and earth at the centre then the wheel of existence, both of the immediate entourage and of the wider commonwealth, could be expected to revolve harmoniously. The all-important aspects of life in the city were an unbroken relation to the centre and a continuity of flow from day to day. The king, the priests, the judges, the civil servants—these were the symbolic persons: the palace, the temple, the court of justice—these were the symbolic buildings: the laws of precedence, of property, of division of labour, of religious obligation—these were the symbolic bonds of a well-ordered city life.

II

Against this general background we can now look at a third notable pattern of imagery in the Bible. Chronologically the early days of simple family life so vividly described in the book of Genesis were succeeded by the tense experiences of the deliverance from Egypt so dramatically portrayed in the early part of the book of Exodus. But the rest of the Pentateuch is largely devoted to the laws and regulations which were found to be necessary for the ordering of the life of the ransomed people of Israel. How many of these were in fact promulgated at Sinai or during the course of the wilderness journey may be open to conjecture—a large proportion seem to be related to the circumstances of a much later period in Israel's history. But the all-important witness of these books and of the later prophetic histories which deal with the settlement in Canaan is that laws and ordinances and provisions for civil rulers and religious officials become essential when the immediate objective of a great act of liberation has been achieved. A freedom gained can all too easily be dissipated unless it is preserved within the walls of a city where each serves the other for the common good.

The establishment of the city did not come to pass easily in Israel. The iron of existence as slaves within a highly organized civilization had entered into men's souls. The prophets in particular were profoundly apprehensive of what might happen if God's chosen people attempted to vie with other nations and set up the trappings of the city-state. Yet it had to come. And ultimately we find the pattern which had already established itself in other parts of the Middle East—king, priest, palace, temple, the administration of justice, the daily sacrifices—all now centred in Jerusalem, the city of the great king. David, still symbolizing memorable aspects of the struggle for freedom, becomes the ideal king-figure though his son approximates more closely to the general pattern of Eastern kingship. The temple retains relics of the desert-tabernacle though it too becomes assimilated to the accepted pattern of city worship. The sacrifices become more elaborate, prayers and praises and lamentations more formal and the total complex of an ordered religious city takes shape.

Let us now look at the way in which this imagery was applied to God and His relations with men. First of all the confession recurs again and again without qualification that God alone is King of all the earth. "The Lord reigns: let the peoples tremble! He sits enthroned upon the cherubim: let the earth quake! Mighty King, lover of justice, thou hast established equity; thou hast executed justice and righteousness in Jacob" (Ps. 99. 1-4, R.S.V.). "The Lord reigns; he is robed in majesty; the Lord is robed, he is girded with strength. Yea, the world is established; it shall never be moved; thy throne is established from of old; thou art from everlasting" (Ps. 93 . 1-2. R.S.V.). "There is none like thee, O Lord; thou art great, and thy name is great in might. Who would not fear thee, O King of the nations? For this is thy due. The Lord is the true God; he is the living God and the everlasting King" (Jer. 10. 6-7, 10. R.S.V.). "The Most High rules the kingdom of men and gives it to whom he will" (Dan. 4. 17, R.S.V.). "I am a great King, says the Lord of hosts, and my name is feared among the nations" (Malachi 1. 14, R.S.V.).

That the God of Israel was King and Judge of all the earth was never doubted by the great Hebrew prophets and psalmists. He who created the world and sustained the movements of the heavenly bodies exercised an everlasting kingdom and ruled in righteousness amongst the sons of men. He who ordered the host of the stars, keeping them in their regular orbits and never allowing a single one to fail, held the nations fast under a similar control and would never allow anarchy to prevail. His relation to His own people is described in a more intimate way. He is indeed the King of His people who judges their cause. But sometimes the prophet or psalmist prefers the term Shepherd, itself a royal title: God is the Shepherd who rules over His people in mercy as well as in judgment, in compassion as well as in discipline. Yet however precisely it may be expressed this is the great affirmation of later Judaism. The God of Israel is King of all the earth. He reigns in righteousness and no man or nation is beyond the outreach of His judgments.

Moreover there is the firm conviction that the Judge and Ruler of all never acts arbitrarily or capriciously. The steady and regular motions of the heavenly bodies are sufficient indication of the orderliness of God's ways. Must it not follow that He who works in nature according to observable laws must also in the moral order follow principles which have been established for ever in the heavens? The emphasis in the Old Testament upon the justice and righteousness and faithfulness and dependability of God is most striking. Whatever else may be open to question it cannot be doubted that the Judge of all the earth will do right. His judgments stand like the strong mountains. His righteousness endures throughout all ages. Above all earthly kingdoms the Lord sits enthroned as King for evermore (Ps. 29. 10).

But is this great King altogether remote from the earthly scene in His majestic transcendence? One of the outstanding features of the Old Testament is its frequent references to the King coming to His own place and to His own people. He comes to Jerusalem, He comes to the Temple. He comes in the person of the High-Priest who acts representatively on behalf of the people. The Psalms celebrate the presence of God in the midst of the city, the city He founded, the city He loves. As the king ascends the hill to the central point of the city, as he comes to the temple and stands in its courts, it is as if the King of glory Himself has entered afresh into possession of His own domain. "For the Lord hath chosen Zion: he hath desired it for his habitation" (Ps. 132. 13).

It is almost impossible for us today to enter imaginatively into the outlook of the successive generations of Israel from the time of David until the period of the Herods. There were many variations between the centuries as well as between different members of the community at any one time. But there was steady agreement that the great King had chosen Jerusalem as the place of His special revelation, the place, as it were, where heaven touched earth and where God and man could commune together. Jerusalem could thus be regarded as the centre of the whole earth: healing influences would flow out from it and to it the nations would at length come to learn the ways of the Lord. Further, there was a sustained conviction that the Temple was the heart of the city's life. Its pattern had been given by God to His chosen servant Moses and in its order and proportion it was modelled upon the heavenly sanctuary itself. The symbols of God's own presence were in it and through the sacrificial system a way of regular and ordered communication was established between God and His people. Finally the ordered hierarchy of king, priesthood, judges and people maintained the rhythm of stable relationships which were essential for the welfare of the whole community.

Clearly there were many vicissitudes in this pattern of ordered life. Wars without and factions within, corrupt rulers and unworthy priests, exile and dispersion, the destruction of the temple and the cessation of the daily sacrifice—all these disrupted the organization of worship and social justice. At times it seemed that the most High had abandoned His city and departed from His sanctuary. The kingly succession was broken, the priesthood languished. But the hope of restoration was never altogether extinguished. Such a Psalm as the 110th reveals the firm confidence that a new kingly figure would sit in the place of honour on Mount Zion and would act as priest in the restored temple. His authority would be derived from God Himself and the pattern of His kingdom would reveal the structure of the eternal Kingdom. When He should be acknowledged as God's vicegerent upon earth and when his city and temple should be recognized as the sacramental locus of God's most holy presence, then the world at large would find a true centre, a true coping-stone of an ordered community life and universal peace would be established among men.

In all this conception, the energizing spirit is the spirit of order and discipline. There is no interest in the Old Testament in a rigid uniformity. It could indeed be claimed that in the days of the wilderness journey the people travelled as a band of brothers under a single leader with the simplest possible provisions for justice between man and man and for sacramental observances between men and God. The leader far surpassed his followers in vision, courage and energy and they were content to be directed in all things by him. But the city loses its distinctive quality if it is organized in this way. The principles of the city's existence are variety-in-unity, harmony-through-co-operation, health-through-rhythmical-movement, beauty-through-proportion. So ideally the life of the city is carried forward in ordered departments, with ordered rhythmical movements, and through the agency of ordered vocational groups. From the centre directions are issued to define these orders and communications constantly go out to energize their particular activities. Similarly reports are directed to the centre supplying information or calling for assistance. So long as there is a constant flow of communication, health is maintained within the total structure of the body corporate. But let there be isolation of a particular section, disruption of a particular rhythm, inflation of a particular group and the whole organization is threatened with disaster.

Only rarely does the Old Testament make specific reference to the Spirit of God in this particular context. The focus of interest is the vicegerent who, either in actuality or in the prophet's vision is appointed by God, exercises His authority and directs (as, for example, in Ezekiel 40 ff) the plan and organization of city and temple and community. Yet if there is to be health and vitality everything in fact depends upon the outflow and inflow of the Spirit, rhythmically and regularly. The pictures of breath pulsating through the human body or of river-waters pouring into the channels of irrigation or of winds sweeping through dank and torpid valleys are most apt. The Spirit works throughout the whole society, first to mediate order from the centre through all the channels leading out to the circumference, then to bring back the sicknesses of the circumference to the healing energies of the centre. In the Old Testament the outline-sketch of the community of the Spirit begins to appear. But in reality the city still waits for its King, and for the outpouring of the Spirit Who alone can establish righteousness and peace.

The earliest confession of faith in Christ according to the record of Acts 2 ended in this way:

> Men and brethren, let me freely speak unto you of the patriarch David, that he is both dead and buried, and his sepulchre is with us unto this day. Therefore being a prophet, and knowing that God had sworn with an oath to him, that of the fruit of his loins, according to the flesh, he would raise up Christ to sit on his throne; he seeing this before spake of the resurrection of Christ that his soul was not left in hell, neither his flesh did see corruption.
>
> This Jesus hath God raised up, whereof we all are witnesses. Therefore being by the right hand of God exalted, and having received of the Father the promise of the Holy Ghost, he hath shed forth this, which ye now see and hear. For David is not ascended into the heavens: but he saith himself, The Lord said unto my Lord, Sit thou on my right hand, Until I make thy foes thy footstool. Therefore let all the house of Israel know assuredly, that God hath made that same Jesus, whom ye have crucified, both Lord and Christ'' (vv. 29-36).

The imagery of this passage is unmistakable. David was the greatest of all the kings in Israel's history. Yet he looked forward to the coming of one whom he called *Lord*. Surely Jesus of Nazareth, raised from the dead, must be the Lord of whom David spoke. He has been exalted to the place of royal authority and has become thereby the channel through whom the promised Spirit has been given to men. David did not ascend into the heavens. But Jesus has ascended and is now the Lord and Kingly Priest of whom the Psalmist speaks in the great 110th Messianic Psalm.

Here at once we have the framework of the New Testament witness to Christ as God's vicegerent and to the Church as the restored and revived Israel. But for the present neither city nor temple appear, though the mention of a throne may be held to imply a city and the reference to the priestly psalm a temple. The emphasis for the present is upon the body which did not see corruption and has been exalted into the heavens. In course of time the image of the body—a beautiful focus of order and proportion—will overshadow both city and temple in describing the relations between Christ and His Church. But for the moment we see the Lord reigning in heaven and inaugurating a new era of the Spirit upon earth. All is of God Who directs the universe in His infinite wisdom and foreknowledge: all is through Christ Who humbled Himself to the depths and was exalted to the place of highest authority: all is communicated to men by the energy of the Holy Spirit Who establishes order and discipline within the new community.

Let us now look in some detail at the New Testament confession of faith in God, Father, Son and Holy Spirit in terms of our third basic pattern of imagery. The confession can be defined as that of faith in God, Sovereign King, Exalted Lord and Holy Spirit of Discipline. Although the actual ascription of kingly names to God is comparatively rare in the New Testament the conviction never falters that God is Sovereign over all things and all people. Occasionally the Greek title *despotes* is used, denoting absolute authority and kingly power. Occasionally the title is expanded to King of kings and Lord of lords, denoting a comprehensive control of all the nations. But usually the emphasis is simply upon the reign of God, a reign which is defined once for all in the

Lord's Prayer as the doing of God's will on earth as it is done in heaven.

In the teaching of Jesus nothing is more prominent than His witness to the reign of God. At the beginning of His ministry, He comes into Galilee proclaiming the good news that the Reign of God is at hand. He discloses to His disciples through parables the secret of the Reign of God. He speaks of the possibility of seeking the Reign of God, of receiving it, of entering into it. He declares that the Reign has come near to men and that some are already pressing into it. He finally pictures the fulfilled passover in the Reign of God when the disciples will eat and drink at His table. The conception moves to and fro between past and future: between heaven and earth: between social and individual: between steady state and active operation. The Reign of God embraces every aspect of life that man can envisage. When God is King, every element of man's existence is brought under His sovereign sway.

In the case of Jesus this was actually and literally true. He lived ever and always, willingly and joyfully, under the sovereign reign of God. This reign becomes "the sphere in which he lives and moves and has his being. His preaching of the Kingdom is not just the pointing of His hearers to some happy state in the future, when the will of God will be perfectly realized; it is primarily the living of a life of complete loyalty to God and unquestioning obedience to His will here and now. The core of all that Jesus teaches about the Kingdom is the immediate apprehension and acceptance of God as King in his own life. From this central experience all the rest of the teaching on the Kingdom naturally follows. The kingdoms of the world with all their glory are not to be weighed against the loyalty that is due to God. 'Thou shalt worship the Lord thy God and Him only shalt thou serve.' So the ministry begins. As it draws towards its close the same voice is heard in the garden: 'Not what I will but what thou wilt.' The best that the world can offer and the worst that it can threaten are alike powerless to divert him from this one allegiance" (T. W. Manson, *The Teaching of Jesus*, p. 161).

Yet it would be wrong to imagine that the Reign is pictured by Jesus simply in terms of a willing submission to God's absolute authority. It is this. But constantly the assurance recurs that the Reign comes near to man in grace and succour. The soul may appear to be a battleground of rival forces, with all kinds of subtle temptations drawing man away from his true allegiance. How then can he be truly obedient to his sovereign King? Yet if the temptations are strong, the grace of the Kingdom drawing near is stronger. Near in space, near in time, near in the social environment, the glorious reign of God exercises its pressure upon men, in and through the simplest and most common-place circumstances of daily life.

This is the inescapable lesson of the parables of Jesus. They focus attention upon the most ordinary situations of the home, the farm, the market, the courts of justice, the open road. Any one of these may constitute a tiny drama of the absolute demand and the unlimited grace of God's Reign. This Reign comes like the seed into the soil: men may welcome it and bring forth fruit, they may resist it and become sterile. It comes like the sudden discovery of the pearl of great price: men may sell all and grasp it or they may pass it by. It comes like the choice between building on a rock or upon the sand: to submit to the authority of God is to be founded on a rock and no storms of life can disturb a life so grounded. But again this choice might seem to involve an intolerable strain were it not that the Reign of God comes near not only through the pressure of these simple events but above all through Him Who interprets the significance of these events and mediates through His own person the very authority and grace which He proclaims.

For another aspect of Jesus' teaching which stands out quite clearly in the Gospels concerns the role which He Himself plays in the Reign of God. In essence He proclaims that through His own ministry—judging and saving, making demands and offering grace—the Reign of God is already and existentially present. He demands nothing less than a wholehearted submission to the will of God: at the same time He stands by the man so challenged and holds at bay the demons of egoism and worldliness which seek to prevent the submission. His own glad obedience is the supreme witness to the glory of the Reign. The authority which He exercises amongst those to whom He speaks marks Him out as one who is the perfect human embodiment of the sovereign rule of God. The standard which He proclaims for life within the Kingdom is the standard by which His own life is constantly guided and fulfilled. The One who perfectly does the will of God has the right to call all men to the same obedience.

In the actual disclosure of what obedience to the will of God implies Jesus establishes a twofold standard: a total devotion to God, unlimited service to the neighbour. This he proceeded to exemplify in his life of social relationships —always devoting Himself first to the Reign of God, always ready to give Himself in ministering to the neighbour. But he framed the same pattern in his life of worship. He offered Himself constantly to God on behalf of His fellows, thus loving God in His neighbour and His neighbour in God. In the noble phrase of the Epistle to the Hebrews it was in an eternal Spirit that He offered Himself without spot to God. The Psalmist's prayer "Lo I come to do thy will, O my God" was made the key-note of His whole career. Symbolically this offering was made when He gave His body to God and to His fellow-men in the broken bread of the Last Supper. In a still more poignant symbolic action the offering was made absolute when He went up willingly to the Cross, still praying that others might be forgiven and saved through His sacrifice.

This reign of God, coming with authority in the life and activity of Jesus Himself, established itself with power in the hearts of men through the continuing work of the Holy Spirit. This aspect of the Spirit's activity receives little specific mention in the Gospels and yet there is at least one example of the Spirit being virtually equated with the exercise of the Reign. Even if Luke's version of the Lord's saying that the casting out of demons by the *finger* of God is the open sign of the coming near of the Reign is the original, Matthew's substitution of Spirit for finger shows how the Spirit was regarded in the early Church (Matt. 12. 28; Luke 11. 20). The setting up of the Reign of God in the hearts of men was the work of the Spirit. The Reign which had been manifested perfectly in the obedience of Jesus was manifested with true authority wherever the Spirit reproduced the saving image of Jesus in the life of the Church. Only gradually was this doctrine developed but its pattern appears at least in principle in the Gospels. Wherever men welcome the reign of God and submit themselves in humility and ordered discipline to His obedience, there the Spirit has been working, the Spirit of the Lord Christ, the Spirit who gathers humble souls into the perfect obedience of Jesus and enables them to offer themselves, their souls and bodies a willing sacrifice to God.

v

Outside the Gospels the imagery of kingship is used most sparingly in the New Testament. It must have been well-known that one of the main charges leading to the condemnation of Jesus by the Roman governor was that He had claimed to be a king. And at a relatively early stage in Paul's missionary activity he and his companion Silas were seized and the accusation levelled against them that they had flouted the Emperor's laws by asserting that there was a rival king, one Jesus. How far all this may have been responsible for the avoidance of kingly terms in speaking of Jesus and his work we cannot know. The early witnesses did not hesitate to acclaim Jesus as 'Lord', a title which certainly implied honour and authority and rulership. But until the conflict between the Church and the Roman power became really acute it seems that it was a comparatively rare thing, particularly in Gentile circles, to proclaim the Kingdom of God or to refer to Jesus as King. The most notable exception is the striking declaration in 1 Corinthians 15 that when the end comes, Jesus the Christ will deliver up the kingdom to God the Father after abolishing every kind of dominion, authority and power. Then God will be all in all.

But in spite of the fact that precise references to king and kingdom are rare, this does not mean that the ideas implicit in this imagery are absent. In fact the key-note of kingship as it develops in the Old Testament is the quality of righteousness and if there is one quality in the relationship between God and man which is central for St. Paul it is that of *righteousness*. In the writings of prophets and psalmists we find the constantly recurring theme that God is the Righteous King, that His anointed representative is the agent of his righteousness amongst men and that it is at the heart of God's purpose that His people shall become righteous too.

> The Lord reigns: let the earth rejoice.
> Righteousness and justice are the foundation of His throne.
> The heavens proclaim His righteousness;
> The daughters of Judah rejoice, because of Thy judgments,
>   O God (Ps. 97. 1, 2, 6, 8, R.S.V.).

Because the eternal King is righteous, his earthly representative must also be righteous.

> Give the king thy justice, O God,
>   and thy righteousness to the royal son!
> May he judge thy people with righteousness,
>   and thy poor with justice (Ps. 72. 1, 2, R.S.V.).

Finally the result will be that if the earthly king is exercising the righteousness of the heavenly King, the people will themselves dwell in righteousness and peace.

> The Lord loves those who hate evil;
> Light dawns for the righteous
>   and joy for the upright in heart.
> Rejoice in the Lord, O you righteous,
>   and give thanks to His holy name (Ps. 97. 10-12, R.S.V.)

St. Paul proclaimed the Christian Gospel against this background of kingly righteousness as found in the Old Testament. The kingdom of God, he wrote, in one of his few explicit references to it, is not meat and drink but righteousness and peace and joy in the Holy Spirit. This is exactly the imagery of Psalm 97. When God is King and when His righteousness is active amongst men, they will themselves dwell in harmony and joy. But this will only happen when the righteousness of God has been revealed and when His judgments have been made known. To show how this has come about in and through the work of Christ and the Holy Spirit is St. Paul's dominant purpose in the Epistle to the Romans.

At the foundation of the Old Testament conception of righteousness is a covenant between two parties by which each is committed to certain obligations. These obligations are of a mutual character, often quite simple, sometimes quite elaborate. In the case of Israel the all-important covenant was sealed after the deliverance from Egypt when God revealed His demands, cultic and ethical, and promised His protection. The people on their part received His gift and pledged their obedience. In a quite simple way God's righteous rule over His people was established and they were assured of a life of righteousness and peace under His care.

But changing circumstances brought new complexities into social life. Those in authority were often tempted to mould the pattern of the nation's institutions upon that of other apparently more successful peoples. The nation itself was ever liable to fail in obedience to the requirements of its own covenant pledge. As a consequence prophets and law-givers proclaimed with renewed emphasis that God rules and judges in righteousness, that his earthly representative, the king, must be righteous too and that the nation could prosper only if every section in the community was careful to fulfil its covenant obligations. Beset by the painful experiences of national defeats and social injustices, they yet hoped that God's righteousness would again be demonstrated in some unmistakable way, that an earthly king would arise who would reign in righteousness according to God's laws, and that the nation at large, having passed through the fires of judgment and having been vindicated openly, would dedicate itself afresh to the pursuit of righteousness in every aspect of its life. The whole of the later history of Judaism moves within the framework of this hope. When will God come forth in righteous judgment to vindicate the good and to destroy the evil? When will a king arise as a faithful dispenser of God's righteousness both in Jerusalem and among the nations? When will humble and penitent souls who wait for God's righteousness be justified and refreshed?

These are questions which can be limited neither to one people nor to one period of history and it was St. Paul's genius to develop, in his letter to Christians living at Rome, the centre of the Gentile world, an interpretation of God's action in Christ which would provide answers to these questions for all nations and all times. The letter is universal in its outreach. The nations of the world are certainly under the judgment of God for whereas they could have seen in the created order the essential principles of harmonious and wholesome behaviour, they refused to be guided by them and abandoned themselves rather to extremes of selfish and sensual conduct. But the Jews are also under judgment for, having been given a codified Law defining their duties and privileges, they failed to honour the Law, interpreted God's forbearance as indifference and settled down to an existence in which conscience was dulled and justice between man and his neighbour was virtually ignored. All the world, therefore, is guilty: none is righteous: all fall short of God's glory: all who are hard and impenitent are storing up for themselves a harvest of wrathful judgment when at the last God reveals His righteousness and divides the evil from the good.

Having thus borne witness to the unchallengeable righteousness of the Divine King and to the inexcusable apostasy of His subjects, St. Paul proceeds to make His utterly startling and paradoxical pronouncement. The Messianic King, Jesus our Lord, has come in righteousness as God's anointed representative but instead of scattering immediately the forces of darkness and establishing a reign of peace, He allowed Himself to be the victim through whom the Divine righteousness could be vindicated without final destruction descending upon the world. St. Paul insists that God has been infinitely patient and forbearing, appearing to pass over the infringements of His righteous order, allowing men to go almost to the limit in their pride and self-indulgence. But now at length He has acted openly, dramatically, definitively. Yet not in direct judgment upon the guilty world. Coming in the likeness of sinful flesh, the Messianic king has absorbed the judgment into his own flesh. Assuming the garments of a sinful humanity, the King has offered himself the perfect expiation on behalf of that humanity. All is of God and is the direct result of His grace. His righteousness has most certainly been revealed but the revelation has been towards salvation not condemnation, towards the justification of man and not his annihilation. God Himself is eternally righteous. But by the marvellous display of the Cross He reveals Himself as the One who puts in the right every one who believes in Jesus, and acknowledges Him as Sin-Bearer and Lord.

VI

This whole conception does not easily make its impact upon those who belong to the tradition and civilization of the West. Over the past four centuries there has been a growing emphasis upon the place of the individual within society and the sense of solidarity, which belonged to ancient cultures and still belongs to those parts of the world relatively untouched by the individualism of the West, has gradually slipped away. Yet there can be no doubt that within the period covered by the Biblical literature the sense of corporateness, as for example between a ruler and his people, was very strong indeed. The people's health depended upon the well-being of the king. The people's justice, the system, that is, in which each member of the community occupied his appropriate place and performed his appointed duties, depended upon the unceasing exercise of the king's authority. What the king was and did was bound to affect for good or ill the whole body corporate and these effects could even be transmitted to generations yet unborn. To use an organic metaphor, if the heart of the organism was functioning normally and effectively, the healing influence would be felt throughout the whole body—and vice versa.

Clearly this understanding of man's corporate existence

underlies St. Paul's view of the Fall and the effect of Adam's sin upon the human race. The universal sinfulness of man, depicted so graphically in the early chapters of the Epistle to the Romans, could stand as an authentic account of the human condition even apart from the later theory of the effect of the sin of Adam upon the human race. But the reference to Adam emphasizes the solidarity of the race in a representative man. What he does as natural head and progenitor is bound to affect all his descendants and St. Paul finds in this thought a confirmation of the universal sinfulness already portrayed.

But if this doctrine of solidarity is true of humanity within the natural order of creation, it is still more true of the redeemed humanity within the gracious order of the new creation. The only difference—and it is a very large one— is that the new creation is constituted on the basis of faith and not of natural birth, of a willed commitment rather than of an automatic heritage. It was due to the will of God mani- festing itself in a stupendous action—"God sending his own Son in a form like that of our own sinful nature, and as a sacrifice for sin" (Romans 8. 3, N.E.B.)—that the way was opened for men to escape from the control of their lower nature, the solidarity in sin by which they were bound, and to be united with the Lord Christ in the new order of the Spirit. The commitment by which they came to be united with the head of this new community was the act of faith. In other words, just as the life of a city has always depended upon the ready willingness of those who desire citizenship to leave behind many of their ordinary *natural* ties and to accept the privileges and duties of a deliberately planned society, so in the new order to which St. Paul bears witness, those who through faith have become united with Christ may be Jew or Gentile, bond or free, male or female—they are all one in Christ Jesus. And being united with Him in this new solidarity they receive all that He has won for them, they respond to the authority which He now exercises over them. As St. Paul puts it in a striking phrase, *they reign* through the one man, Jesus Christ.

The images and the ideas of the Epistle to the Romans are so vivid and so challenging that it is impossible to formulate any straightforward system of doctrine which will embrace them all. But every leading doctrine of the faith, with the possible exception of the doctrine of the Eucharist, may be found in this remarkable book and the dominant pattern of imagery which holds them together is, I believe, that of the King of Righteousness sending His Messianic vicegerent to right the wrongs of the earthly scene and to inaugurate a new order of righteousness and peace. The universal sin of mankind is seen as a refusal to honour God and to obey His laws: the universal consequence of sin as degradation and death. The supreme act of the King's grace is the sending of His royal son to live under the conditions of a sinful humanity, bound by the Law and by Death. The supreme act of the Son is His submission to death as a sacrifice for sin, to the shedding of His blood as a means of reconciliation. Because of His complete solidarity with those whom He represented, His act was their act at least potentially. But this potentiality could not become actual save through the Spirit. Not by automatic incorporation but by Spirit-inspired identification it was now open to man to confirm his union with Christ in His life-pattern—His sufferings, His death, His resurrection. This identification was made in the act of baptism when believers were buried with Christ in His death, in order that as Christ was raised from the dead by the glory of the Father they too might walk in newness of life. But this new creation was all the time dependent upon the Spirit, the Spirit poured out by Jesus, the Spirit who delights to weave the pattern of Jesus' own life into the very fabric of human existence.

This is the outline of Christian doctrine as sketched in the Epistle to the Romans. The Grace of God is primary, the faith of man follows. This faith would have been impossible, unless God in His royal grace had taken the initiative. Yet this faith is a willed response to what God has done. And it is faith energized by the Holy Spirit. No form of words can entirely resolve the paradox that in every response I make to the initiative of God, it is I who respond and yet it is not I but the grace of God working with me: it is I who seek to be united with Christ in His death and resurrection and yet it is not I but the Holy Spirit bearing witness with my spirit. Faith is ultimately a mystery and no analysis of a philosophical or psychological kind can exactly define its operation. Yet faith is a reality and the citizens of the city of God are those who have transcended all natural structures by committing themselves to the Christ in trust and obedience through the directing agency of the Holy Spirit.

VII

I believe in the Holy Spirit. No one has ever made this affirmation with greater conviction or as a result of deeper personal experience than St. Paul. The life-giving law of the Spirit sets man free from the law of sin and death. The God who raised Jesus from the dead gives new life to man's mortal body through his indwelling Spirit. Those who are led by the Spirit are not under law. Where the Spirit of the Lord is, there is liberty. Such statements reveal his assurance that God, Who had acted so graciously and so wondrously in Christ, was continuing and would continue that work through the Spirit (Who is interchangeably the Spirit of God and the Spirit of the Lord Christ) in the hearts of men.

It is possible to define many aspects of the Spirit's work. But in the particular area of imagery in which we have moved in this chapter, we think of the Holy Spirit as supremely the Spirit of order and harmony, the Spirit Who brings every manifestation of life back to the control of the central authority who is the Lord Christ. The dominant pictures are those of a city and of a temple and of a living organism. In each case there is a central focus from which channels of communication lead out to give directions to and receive messages from the manifold parts which make up the whole. Particularly is this the case with the human body which, as St. Paul points out more than once, has many members each with its own function to perform and which needs therefore a principle of order to ensure the harmonious working of the whole. In the case of the Christian community which is likened now to a city, now to a temple, but most strikingly of all to a body, the same conclusion must be drawn. It must have a co-ordinating principle and that principle, according to St. Paul, is provided by the living Spirit of God Who operates in every part within the pattern of wholeness which is that of the Lord Christ Himself.

This conception obviously grows out of what Paul had

known in Judaism but goes far beyond it. As I have already shown, the community of God's faithful people under the Old Covenant was established at Sinai when God's gracious initiative in choosing this people was met by a response in a ritual act (signifying a whole-hearted devotion to God Himself) and in a promise of ethical obedience. Later in the more settled period of their history the Hebrews still sought to make their responses through ordered ritual acts and detailed ethical obedience. But Paul, despairing of making any kind of ultimate response in these ways, believed that what had been impossible within a strictly formalized system of ritual and ethical laws, could become possible within a new order whose energizing power was the Spirit of the Lord Christ Himself. In God's New Covenant the sacrifice of Christ, not the Law, became the essential link between God and man. The response from man's side consisted not in following a code of ritual and ethics which tended to grow ever more detailed and complex but in accepting Christ as Lord and in allowing His Spirit to make obedience to that Lordship actual in every department of his life.

This did not mean, however, that in the new order there would be no place for regulated worship and disciplined conduct. The Church of the New Covenant, the Church re-constituted by the sacrifice of Christ, was already the adumbration of the city of God, the new Jerusalem. Its citizens are those who have been baptized into the name of Jesus and have acknowledged Him as Lord and received His mark upon their foreheads. Thereby they have committed themselves to a life of ordered worship and disciplined service through which God will be glorified and the pattern of the fellowship of the Spirit will be manifested to the world.

The nature of the life of worship is depicted through imagery taken from the temple and priesthood and sacrifices of the Old Testament sanctuary. In the period of the New Testament, conditions did not allow the construction of symbolic shrines for worship—the community of Christians was itself the spiritual temple built of living stones (1 Peter 2. 5). The whole people of God constituted a royal priesthood under the one High Priest and although representative men must have performed special duties within this priesthood, the New Testament does not indicate how this was organized or arranged. The clearest imagery is that associated with sacrifice, for the royal priesthood offers spiritual sacrifices acceptable to God through Jesus Christ and those who have been justified within the righteousness of Jesus Christ are called to offer themselves a living sacrifice to God, this being the form of worship altogether acceptable to Him. On the basis of the New Testament evidence alone it is impossible to associate this sacrificial worship in any formal way with the celebration of the Lord's Supper. All we can infer is that the Supper, being the central act by which the community recalled the Lord's own sacrifice, must have provided a unique occasion for the offering of the sacrificial worship which was the bounden duty of the royal priesthood. Their royal High Priest was, they knew, ministering for ever in the heavenly sanctuary. They, on earth, could continually offer up the sacrifice of praise in dependence upon the Spirit Who is for ever sanctifying the things of earth by lifting them up to heaven.

The nature of the Christian's ethical obedience is depicted

through imagery taken from the city and its officials and the prescribed duties of its citizens. Here the matter is more complicated than in the sphere of worship for provision has to be made for a dual set of obligations—on the one side to the secular authorities and on the other side to the authority of the Lord Christ, exercised over those who are citizens of the heavenly kingdom. As regards the former no encouragement is given to general disobedience or anarchy. Christians are called to submit themselves to every human institution for the sake of the Lord—to the sovereign, to the governor, to rulers, to employers, to tax officials. If at any time a human institution should attempt to seize *absolute* power, then as the Book of the Revelation of St. John shows, there must be a firm and fearless resistance. But so long as government institutions concern themselves with the ordering of social life, justice between man and man and conditions of general security, the Christian can accept obligations laid upon him as having their sanction in the discipline of the Divine Kingdom itself.

Within the area of the Church's own specialized existence there is also the need for submission to those who exercise authority in the name of Christ and for service in disciplined ways on behalf of the common brotherhood. No uniformity of ecclesiastical order can be distinguished in the New Testament but apostles, presbyters and teachers certainly acted as human representatives of the Lord Himself and the harmonious working of the community depended upon their faithfulness in the exercise of their responsibilities. But perhaps even more important than obedience to the directions of church-rulers was the acceptance by every church-member of his duty to serve his fellow-citizen in the

heavenly kingdom. The classic imagery by which this obligation is illuminated is that of the body and its members. "God
has combined the various parts of the body, giving special
honour to the humbler parts, so that there might be no
sense of division in the body, but that all its organs might
feel the same concern for one another. If one flourishes,
they all rejoice together" (1 Cor. 12. 24-26, N.E.B.). But
it would not be difficult to suggest a similar model for the
harmonious functioning of the life of a city. Mutual respect
and tolerance, mutual service and co-operation—these are
incumbent upon the Christian just because he is a servant of
the Lord Who is fashioning the city and the kingdom
according to the pattern laid up in heaven.

Christian life during the period between the Lord's
ascension to His seat of authority and the eventual yielding
up of His completed work to the eternal King, involves
ordered worship and disciplined service here on earth. But
all this is to be regarded only as the foretaste and the fore-
shadowing of the perfect worship and the perfect mutuality
of love which characterize the heavenly city. Nowhere is the
heavenly city more vividly portrayed than in the Revelation
of St. John. The city is perfect in its proportions and in its
harmonies of colour and sound. It is radiant with light,
vibrant with life. It contains nothing that is unwholesome
or unclean. "The throne of God and of the Lamb will be
there, and his servants shall worship him; they shall see him
face to face and bear his name on their foreheads. There
shall be no more night, nor will they need the light of lamp
or sun, for the Lord God will give them light; and they shall
reign for evermore" (Rev. 22. 3-5, N.E.B.). Through the
ages God's elect have had no permanent home, having

always been seekers after the city which is to come. At times when a great company has been lifted heavenwards in some notable experience of corporate worship, when a community has enjoyed a rich sense of fellowship through participating in some common outpouring of service, then the form of the city has already begun to appear. But its perfection is beyond the bounds of space and time. The Church is not the City nor the Kingdom nor ever can be. But in the Church the glory begins to be revealed and men rejoice in hope of its fulfilment in the city which hath foundations whose builder and maker is God.

Chapter Six

DISCIPLES OF THE TRUTH

FROM the home to the frontier, from the frontier to the city: is there any further obvious stage in man's pilgrimage here on earth? At first sight it might appear that the final goal would be the establishment of some kind of international control—a council or league of nations, an international court of justice, an assembly authorized to enforce order everywhere in the world. History records the rise and fall of many empires, each of which has dreamed of exercising authority over the inhabited world. May it not then ultimately come about that a universal community *will* be established and that the lives of all men will be directed by a single rule?

This may indeed come to pass. But if it does, this will only be the expansion of the city-ideal to its limits. Man will not thereby be concerned with fresh aspects of his individual and corporate existence. A radically new development will only come to pass if the concern for order is followed by the search for *meaning*. There may have been reasonable freedom to explore, there may have been a general willingness to co-operate in the construction of the city. But unless these activities begin to be seen within the context of a pattern of *significance*—ultimately within the context of universal *meaning*—they will be lacking in any permanent value. The struggle for freedom may be exciting but unless it is directed towards a goal which makes sense of the energy expended it gradually loses its incentive and finally peters out. The building of the city may inspire loyalty and even sacrifice but unless it is related to a meaningful end interest soon wanes and men prepare to settle for any kind of relative stability.

So we find another institution appearing in human history. Generally speaking it has been concerned to draw together the results of all man's known experiments in living, to encourage the search for a pattern of meaning which will serve to integrate these results and to promote within this framework further developments in individual and social life. This institution has received various names—the school, the academy, the college, the institute. But the name which symbolizes the widest outreach both in persons involved and in subjects studied is *university*. The university, at least ideally, seeks to gather into one place a widely representative community of scholars and they in turn seek to gather into one curriculum a universal body of knowledge.[1] The

[1] cf. an interesting passage in a sermon preached by Professor C. A. Coulson in the University Church at Oxford on October 14th, 1962.

"We live and work within the framework of a university. Here is the claim, made effectively nowhere else but in a university, that the world makes sense; that it makes *one* sense, and not a lot of separate senses. We are not cultivating, each one of us, our little parcel of ground, our own allotment, quite untroubled and uninterested by what goes on in neighbouring plots. We are entering a rich heritage which we accept for ourselves and which we are trying to extend. Here indeed is, what someone called, 'the altogetherness of everything' which alone justifies us in speaking of ourselves as a uni-versity. Here, if we keep our eyes open, we realise that you can't be a scientist without being a philosopher, you can't be a philosopher without being a historian, or a historian without being a sociologist, or a sociologist without being a psychologist, or a psychologist without being a scientist. The world is one, and the knowledge that is in it is one—because God made it so, and for no other reason; it is his hallmark that is stamped upon it."

very word school carries over from its Greek original the idea of leisure and it is only when conditions are such as to allow certain members of the community to be relieved of some of the ordinary duties of social life that the work of scholarship can go forward. That such work is essential to the well-being of society has rarely been denied. To use a striking simile of the 16th century, the universities are the *eyes* of the land. If the eyes of a society are put out or even blinkered, that society begins to stumble and ultimately falls. In the words of an oft-quoted verse of the Old Testament: "Where there is no vision, the people perish."

I

The Hebrews, by virtue of the changes and chances of their historical existence, had little opportunity to establish a centre of learning which could merit the name 'university'. But the geographical position of Palestine was such that contact with the chief centres of learning in the ancient world must have been frequent. The wisdom of Egypt was proverbial: the cosmologies of the Babylonians and Assyrians were famous: and before the end of the Old Testament period the ideas of the Persians and the learning of the Greeks were filtering into the Hebrew consciousness. In a certain sense the Hebrew seers themselves constituted a focus of international learning for although they were constantly resisting the ideas which came from abroad, in the very act of resistance they were learning from them. Their own God and His covenant were to be set in an ever-expanding context as a result of the movements of the nations and the very stimulus of painful encounter with other peoples helped the prophets and wise men of Israel to press forward in the search for an ultimate pattern of meaning.

By the time of David and Solomon the kingdom was firmly established and the God of Israel was acknowledged as the Lord of Hosts, the strong Rock of his people's salvation. Almost certainly a body of laws existed by which the religious and ethical life of the nation could be governed but it is unlikely that this was extensive in scope or that it was regarded as applying to those outside the borders of Israel. Yet as contacts with other peoples continued and the fortunes of God's elect rose and fell, prophets began to look to much wider horizons and to approach the conception of a God Who not only ruled His own people according to a given standard of righteousness but Who also extended His sovereignty over other nations and governed them according to the same basic principles of justice. Then in the 6th century B.C. Jerusalem fell. The best of the people were deported to an alien land where they began to have contact with a culture whose intellectual accomplishments went far beyond anything they had hitherto known. So the way was prepared for prophets to bear witness to a God Who not only ruled the nations of the earth in righteousness but who also directed the total operation of the universe by laws of His own devising. The final result was that during the half-millenium preceding the advent of Christ the leading minds of Israel were producing a body of testimonies, ultimately to be formulated as Holy Scripture, in which they claimed the whole of mankind for their God and exalted Him as creator and preserver of the whole universe.

In the world's centres of reflection and learning two

matters were of paramount importance. The first concerned the *moral* world of good and evil. How could these be distinguished? Whence had evil come? How could just laws of retribution and reward be established? And what was the explanation of the apparent discrepancies in the working of these laws? In particular when there had been breaches of the moral law how could harmony be restored? The second concerned the *physical* world of life and death. How could these be distinguished? How had mortality come into the world and how could it be held at bay? Could the desert or the dry bones of a nation be restored? These are universal problems and in attempting to grapple with them the prophets and wise men of Israel stepped out into the arena of international debate and began to express their particular faith in universal terms.

In the first place they proclaimed with no uncertain voice that their God, the God of Israel, is high above all other gods and the nations which depend upon them. He is the God of universal justice and righteousness who will by no means clear the guilty, wherever they may be. When sins of inhumanity and gross injustice are committed He acts in judgment, though if men repent and cease from their evil ways He delights in mercy. As for the gods of the nations they are nothing other than lifeless idols. But the affairs of all peoples are under the control of the Holy One of Israel. He is the first and the last. He calls even a heathen emperor to perform His will. But all is for the sake of His righteousness, the triumph of good over evil, which victory He intends to establish in every part of His kingdom.

In the second place they proclaimed that their God, the

Holy One of Israel, is the Creator of all things, the Lord in whose hands are the issues of life and death.

> It is he who sits above the circle of the earth,
> and its inhabitants are like grasshoppers;
> who stretches out the heavens like a curtain,
> and spreads them like a tent to dwell in;
> who brings princes to nought,
> and makes the rulers of the earth as nothing.
> The Lord is the everlasting God,
> the Creator of the ends of the earth.
>
> (Isa. 40. 22-3, 28, R.S.V.).

> I made the earth,
> and created man upon it;
> it was my hands that stretched out the heavens,
> and I commanded all their host (Isa. 45. 12, R.S.V.).

This is the assurance of the prophet and it was echoed by the psalmist and the story-teller. Such a psalm as the 104th proclaims the glory of the Creator and Preserver of all things. Such a story as Genesis 1 imagines the stages through which the primal act of creation was accomplished. All are agreed—prophet, psalmist, story-teller and wise man—that the heavens and the earth constitute one universe, that it was created by the one God in the beginning, that it is being carried forward by this same God towards its true end.

II

With the twofold supremacy of the one God firmly established, the question was bound to arise whether man could obtain detailed knowledge of the nature of His control, moral and physical, of the universe. Were His judgments and His creative actions arbitrary or did they conform to any revealed pattern? To this question the post-exilic Hebrew teachers gave an unequivocal answer. It was through the Law that the nature of God's judgments had been revealed and it was through the pattern expressed in His word that the universe had been created. The Law in its original form had been given to Moses on the mount. It had been preserved and expanded. It had provided a standard by which all men were to be judged and none could keep the righteous judgments of God except by steadfast obedience to it. Further it was through the Word of God—and in time this word came to be virtually equated with the Law—that the heavens were made. "He spake and it was done; He commanded and it stood fast." Thus in the later developments of Judaism God was exalted as transcendent above all nations and above all created things. At the same time He was believed to have graciously revealed the pattern of His moral and physical Lordship through the Law which He had given to Israel. The faithful Jew confessed God as supreme in both the moral and physical orders. He confessed also that God had revealed the nature of His activities in each of these realms through the Law which He had given to His chosen people.

Is it possible to go further still and to find in Judaism the recognition of God's activity both in the hearts of men and in the inner structures of nature itself? Here the evidence is scanty and it is not possible to speak with confidence. Two figures are reasonably prominent and their appearance suggests that men were at least feeling after some expression of the immanence of God. These are

Spirit and Wisdom. In a few cases the Spirit or Breath of God is pictured as operating within the natural or moral order to create new life and to renew the hearts of men. More frequently it is the figure of Wisdom that is described. In the famous passage Proverbs 8. 22 ff Wisdom is called a master-workman, carrying out the designs that God had made with joy. In other parts of the Wisdom literature, it is Wisdom who reveals the way of life and righteousness to men. Sometimes Wisdom is virtually identified with the Law and its functions become the same as those of the Word.

There is therefore no uniformity in the language by which the wise men of later Judaism bore witness to God's activity in the world and in human society. They were sure that He did not work at random: what He did was according to a careful plan which might be called the Word of God, the Law of God or the Wisdom of God. Moreover what He did was brought to its final effectiveness through a powerful agency which might be called the Spirit of God, sometimes the Word of God and sometimes the Wisdom of God. These figures were vividly portrayed and at times personified (this is specially the case with Wisdom). A vocabulary and an imagery were coming into existence and these would prove of immense value to those responsible for bearing witness later to the Christian revelation.

I have spoken of the witness of God as sole Creator and Moral Ruler, a witness which gained enormously in range of vision in the period following the exile. But paradoxically enough, this very expansion made the problems of theodicy ever more acute. If God were so high exalted and so majestic in His creative power, how was it possible to explain the grip of moral evil, the sufferings of the righteous, the inescapability of disease and death? These again are problems which have caused deep anxiety to men in all parts of the world and it is rare to find a philosophical or religious system which does not take the problems of moral evil and human mortality seriously.

Few writings of the Old Testament are more significant than those of the wrestlers with truth who in the post-exilic period tried to maintain on the one hand the majestic power and goodness of an all-wise Creator and on the other hand to deal realistically with the ravages of cosmic disasters, human cruelties, painful disease and sudden death. Nothing is more splendid than the faith of these men, often haltingly and tentatively expressed, that even through human suffering God's wise purpose is being fulfilled and that even over death His creative energy will rise triumphant. Symbolic figures emerge, individual and corporate, who in and through their sufferings remain faithful to God and thereby bring blessing to their fellow-men. Can it be that the quintessential pattern of the Wisdom of God is *new life through suffering and death*? Can it be that it is the Spirit of God working in men's hearts Who reproduces the pattern in their lives and makes them victorious over every tribulation? Can it be that this same Spirit of God is ever seeking to reveal to men that the inner meaning of their existence is vicarious suffering and a relationship with God which transcends death itself? The questions were becoming clarified. The way was being prepared for the outburst of assured testimony which the New Testament brings.

The writers of the New Testament had all been grounded in the faith of Judaism and therefore took for granted the belief that there is one God "from whom are all things and for whom we exist" (1 Cor. 8. 6, R.S.V.). "By faith we understand that the world was created by the word of God so that what is seen was made out of things which do not appear" (Heb. 11. 3, R.S.V.). "It is the God who said 'Let light shine out of darkness' who has shone in our hearts" (2 Cor. 4. 6). We hear the echoes of the great Creation story of Genesis 1 and they suggest that no one dreamed of questioning what was to become (if it had not already become) the Sabbath prayer of the synagogue:

> Blessed art thou, O Lord
> The Most High God,
> Maker of heaven and earth.

In the teaching of Jesus there are frequent and assured references to the world as God's creation and to the life of nature as revealing His constant care. As Günther Bornkamm finely says: "Jesus develops no theory about the beginning of the world, nor does he present an interpretation of the first chapter of the Bible. Of course he can on one occasion make use of the language of the creation narrative (Mark 10. 6 ff) and he shares with every Jew the Old Testament faith in God the Creator and Lord, who called creation into being, cares for it and governs it. But creation does not become a topic of speculation for Jesus. Rather the creation itself is immediately present in his words, in the form in which we all have it before our eyes, there in front of us, in each individual creature. . . Birds and lilies are witnesses of the divine care which makes a mockery of our worries. Not a sparrow falls to the ground without the will of your father. Seed, growth and harvest speak of God's promise, lightning, rain and storm of his judgment. . . The world is seen in the light of the rule and will of God. Thus it becomes a parable and manifests itself as creation" (*Jesus of Nazareth* pp. 117-120).

In the witness of the early Church specific references to creation and providence are few but such as appear are the more impressive as they reveal how unquestioned was the belief in the perfection of God's creative work. To the simple folk at Lystra, Paul and Barnabas proclaimed "a living God who made the heaven and the earth and the sea and all that is in them. . . He did not leave himself without witness (i.e., in past generations) for he did good and gave you from heaven rains and fruitful seasons, satisfying your hearts with food and gladness" (Acts 14. 15, 17, R.S.V.). To the intellectuals of Rome, Paul proclaimed the God who has revealed to all men what can be known about his nature: "ever since the creation of the world his invisible nature, namely, his eternal power and deity, has been clearly perceived in the things that have been made" (Rom. 1. 20, R.S.V.). The *how* of creation and providence is not in any of these passages matter for discussion. It is sufficient to bear witness to a transcendent God Who, as the doxology of the Apocalypse puts it, is worthy

to receive glory and honour and power,
for thou didst create all things
and by thy will they existed and were created.

But when these grand simplicities have been assumed, some of the most difficult problems in the whole of Christian theology begin to appear. They are not essentially different from those of later Judaism to which I have already referred. But they become acute to an unparalleled degree through the career of Jesus, teaching, healing, suffering, dying, rising again and diffusing His Spirit in a new community. How could human lips explain the bitter opposition of evil, human and domestic, with which Jesus had to deal? How account for the sufferings and shameful death of one who had so obviously been in trustful relationship with the Creator and Ruler of all? If He really was God's Messiah and had inaugurated a new age, how was this new world related to that which had been erected in the original providence of God? And if the Spirit had indeed been poured out, how was it that so much travail and suffering remained in the created order, apparently unrelieved? Some of the most splendid theological affirmations of the New Testament concern themselves with these pressing questions. We shall consider in turn their witness concerning (a) The Person and Work of Christ; (b) The Spirit and the Church; (c) The Life Everlasting.

IV

a. *The Person and Work of Christ*

Man has always found one of his highest satisfactions in creating something new—in wood or clay or stone. In the process two essential elements are interwoven—a mental image of that which is to be fashioned and the careful manipulation of some chosen material to form the finished article. It is not surprising that early Christian witnesses tended to think of God's creative work in similar terms.

That the one true God was the originator of all that exists went without saying. But according to what pattern did He execute His work? Certainly it was neither haphazard nor arbitrary—it clearly followed some design. But how could this design be identified? As I have already indicated the Jews, when faced with this question, developed the idea of an intermediary principle called alternatively the Word or the Wisdom of God. Then later, in the attempt to become still more specific, the Divine Wisdom was equated with the Torah or total system of Law of the Hebrew tradition. The study of the Law was the means of learning Wisdom and the place of Wisdom in the divine creative process came easily to be transferred to the Law. In the striking words of Edwyn Bevan, the Law came to be regarded as the incarnation of a cosmic principle.

Such ideas as these form an impressive background to the teaching of New Testament theologians. According to this teaching, the design in the mind of the Creator from the beginning had been *the Word* and this Word had become incarnate in Jesus the Christ. Between God and man there was one true mediator, the man Christ Jesus, Who was Himself in His eternal being the Word and Wisdom of God. The same truth, formulated in a different way, asserts that Jesus the Christ is *the Image* of the invisible God and holds the primacy over all created things. "In Him all things were created, in heaven and on earth, visible and invisible . . . all things were created through him and for him" (Col. 1. 16, R.S.V.). This can mean nothing less than that before the existence of all created orders of being in space and time there was in the eternal nature of God a living pattern or design. This pattern may be named the Wisdom or the Word or the Image or the Light of God. It is the cosmic principle through which the whole creation came into being. But, said the early Christians, daringly yet confidently, this principle has been revealed to us in *personal* terms. It is not the Torah that is the essential word and wisdom of God. The Torah was given as a temporary expedient through Moses. But it is Jesus the Christ Who is the true image and word of the living God. It is the same God Who in the original act of creation commanded light to shine out of darkness who has shined into our hearts to give the light of the knowledge of the glory of God in the face of Jesus Christ.

The most extensive exposition of this theme is to be found in the Prologue of St. John's Gospel. These verses present a formidable problem to the interpreter and much depends upon the background of language and ideas against which they need to be set. It is the contention of Dr. C. H. Dodd in his book *The Interpretation of the Fourth Gospel* that the prologue, while making good sense if 'the Word' is understood in a dominantly Hebraic way, is best understood when set against the background of Hellenistic Judaism, particularly as mediated by Philo. For him *the Word* "is not simply the *uttered* word or command of God; it is the meaning, plan or purpose of the universe, conceived as transcendent as well as immanent, as the thought of God, formed within the eternal Mind and projected into objectivity. From the human point of view it is a rational content of thought, expressed in the order of the universe but it is this, not as with the Stoics, in the sense that the order of the universe is self-originated, self-contained and self-

142

explanatory, but in the sense that its order and meaning express the mind of a transcendent creator" (p. 277).

If this is a correct interpretation of the Word as used in the Prologue, then the great affirmation "The Word became flesh" strikes home with immense power. Quoting again from Dodd's exposition:

"The incarnation of the Logos appears as the final concentration of the whole creative and revealing thought of God, which is also the meaning of the universe, in an individual who is what humanity was designed to be in the divine purpose, and therefore is rightly called the 'Son of Man' " (p. 282).

It is the purpose of the Fourth Gospel to bear witness to the appearance upon the stage of history of the Word Who is the pre-existent *meaning* of the whole universe. The relations of the Word with God on the one side and the world on the other side are perfectly mirrored in those of the Word Incarnate, Who is the Son of Man. The evangelist assumes that the cosmos possesses a divine meaning which it derives from the eternal purpose of God. The uniquely wonderful thing which he proceeds to do is to show what that meaning is by referring directly and in detail to the life and death and resurrection of Jesus, the Son of Man.

v

But in sharp contrast to the light and the glory of the perfect image of God we see a world shrouded in darkness by reason of that which is called "the sin of the world". The revelation of the meaning of the universe and of the pattern of human life, a revelation which came to be so adequately expressed in the career of Jesus, has been clouded by the resistance of men who rejected this *personal* revelation and sought satisfaction rather in their own achievements and their own interpretations. They love darkness rather than light: they prefer their own solutions to the world's problems to that abiding meaning which is expressed in the one word 'Love'. To choose hate rather than love, death rather than life, darkness rather than light—this is the sin of the world and it is sin which both defaces the creation and distorts the true image of man.

At all costs the meaning of the whole created order must be once for all displayed in striking and even startling fashion. The Word becoming flesh is startling enough: but the incarnate Word being lifted up and breaking into glory in the very moment of the uplifting—this is the final and all-inclusive revelation of the plan and purpose of God. Like a musical composition, the Fourth Gospel contains a single phrase or theme which recurs again and again. *The Son of Man must be lifted up*. This lifting up was foreshadowed in the famous healing episode of the Hebrews' wilderness journey when men found salvation by looking towards that which had been lifted up in their midst. The Son of Man when lifted up would draw men of all nations to himself. They would see vividly, surprisingly, that the true meaning of life is self-sacrifice not self-preservation. They would see that the meaning and promise of the whole universe is new life through willingly-accepted death. They would see that suffering and death, as symbolized in the 'lifting up', were to be regarded not as something apart from God but rather as something in which God Himself shares and through which He transfigures the whole pattern of human existence.

This however is not the only symbol by which the meaning and purpose of life are interpreted in the Gospel. Manna had been provided in the wilderness to satisfy physical hunger: the true bread had come from heaven in the in-carnate body of the Son of Man and this body was to be given for the true life of the world. A shepherd had led the people through the days of wilderness wandering: the true Shepherd had come into the world and He would lay down His very life for the sheep. Above all in the drama of the feet-washing, when the Son of Man rose from supper and laid aside His garments and girded Himself with a towel and performed the most menial of all tasks, a pattern was given once and for all of love in action, love which is the ultimate meaning of life. Love stops at nothing. Love stoops to the depths. Love accepts the entail of the past. Love opens a new door into the future. Love expressing itself in the ultimate sacrifice is the meaning of the whole created order. God and man are together in sacrifice and through sacrifice the truth of all things is revealed.

Language strains and almost breaks in the Fourth Gospel as the author seeks to proclaim that Jesus is at one with the Father in the conception, the communication and the diffusion of this ultimate truth. Jesus came from God: He was with God at the very beginning: He shared the glory of God before the world began: He is the Son of God in a relationship which is eternal. Coming into the world He worked unceasingly in perfect harmony with the Father: He did always those things that pleased Him: He bore witness untiringly to the Truth: He dwelt in a relationship of unbroken love with the Father and manifested that love to all whom the Father had given Him. Finally He consecrated Himself to the extension of the revelation into the future. As the Father had sent Him, so He sent forward His disciples: as the Spirit of truth had united Jesus with the Father, so this same Spirit would unite the disciples with Jesus: as the Father loved the Son continuously and the Son the Father, so the disciples being gathered into the love of the Son would dwell in the love of the Father. In the most categorical affirmation of all Jesus says: "My Father and I are one" and the implications, as the Gospel shows, are: one in the Spirit, one in the Truth, one in Sacrificial Love, one in the communication of the whole meaning and purpose of life. This is as far as the language of the Gospel takes us whatever may have been the attempts of later systems of thought to expound the revelation in more detailed ways.

Additional metaphors may be found in other writings of the New Testament but the essential witness is the same. God is Light in His eternal being: the Son is the effulgence of that Light: He is, in other words, the perfect expression under the conditions of earthly existence of the ultimate Light which is ultimate Meaning. God is Life in His eternal being: the Son is the word of that Life: He is the word that was spoken into the world: He is, in fact, the perfect communication under the conditions of earthly existence of human life as God designed it to be. God is Love in His eternal being: the Son is the expression of that Love: He is the Love that came into the world: He is the perfect actualization under human conditions of the love which is

146

the ultimate nature of God and the ultimate meaning of all that exists.

One other image is peculiarly characteristic of the writings of St. Paul: it is that of *reconciliation*. This is perhaps the most comprehensive single word of the New Testament for it tries to gather within its embrace the original creation, the estrangement caused by evil in all its forms, and the restoration brought about through the work of God in Christ. In one crucial statement we read "God was in Christ reconciling the world to Himself" (2 Cor. 5. 19); in another "Through Him God chose to reconcile the whole universe to Himself" (Col. 1. 20, N.E.B.). Yet Paul has already declared that in the Son everything in heaven and on earth was created. How then could there be the need of reconciliation? To this question Paul never gives a strictly logical answer. He is content to affirm that all men shared in Adam's disobedience and thereby the whole human race became estranged from God and subject to the final symbol of estrangement, namely physical death. Moreover this condition was not confined to the human race. The whole created order was affected and a state of futility reigned in the whole universe.

But he through whom all men and all things were created, identified himself voluntarily with the estranged universe. Because it had been created in his image, he could identify himself with it in its totality, apart that is from the sin and death by which it had been corrupted. Yet in His superabundant love He even took upon Himself the load of sin and death and annulled it in His own crucifixion and resurrection. Man and the universe need still to enter into the enjoyment of this reconciliation but from

God's side the all-inclusive act has been accomplished. The meaning of the universal process has been revealed once and for all. It is that the created order should gather up into itself even its own contradiction and become the reconciled order. Or, from another angle, it is that the meaning of the universe should gather up into itself even its own contradiction and that the 'Yes' of God should be seen in its fullest glory as it includes the 'No' of men and nature within the final summing up of all things in Christ.

We are left in no doubt that the great theological interpreters of the New Testament see in Jesus of Bethlehem and Calvary and the Empty Tomb the incarnation of the living God Himself. They believe that in Him was manifested the pattern of meaning which had existed from all eternity in the mind of God and that in Him even the contradiction of this meaning was gathered up into a new order of reconciliation. That the Son should be revealed in glory was the purpose of universal creation: that He should through acceptance of the contradictions of this creation ascend to an even higher glory was the meaning of universal reconciliation.

VI

b. *The Holy Spirit and the Church*

In the realm of imagery within which we are now moving the Holy Spirit is supremely the Interpreter, the Spirit of truth. This implies, to use a fine phrase of Paul Tillich's, that "to live spiritually is to live in the presence of meaning". Transposing this a little and relating it to the witness of the New Testament we might say: "To live in the Spirit is to be led into ever deeper meaning"—the meaning of what St. Paul calls God's hidden wisdom, his secret purpose framed from the very beginning to bring us to our full glory. For "things beyond our seeing, things beyond our hearing, things beyond our imagining, all prepared by God for those who love him" these have been revealed to us by God through His Spirit. In striking words St. Paul continues: "The Spirit explores everything, even the depths of God's own nature. Among men, who knows what a man is but the man's own spirit within him? In the same way, only the Spirit of God knows what God is. This is the Spirit that we have received from God, and not the Spirit of the world, so that we may know all that God of his own grace gives us; and, because we are interpreting spiritual truths to those who have the Spirit, we speak of those gifts of God in words found for us not by our own human wisdom but by the Spirit" (1 Cor. 2. 7-13, N.E.B.).

The whole context of this remarkable passage shows that the revelation of God's wisdom in history has been made in Christ and his Cross. But the interpretation of that event, the unveiling of its innermost truth, the relating of it to the essential nature of God Himself—this is the work of the Spirit. The Spirit illumines men's minds and gives them means to bear witness to what they have seen. In this area of imagery the Church is the company of those who have received the Spirit of truth and are being led by Him to an ever deepening apprehension of God's revelation in Christ.

This is exactly the emphasis of the famous Paraclete passages in John 14-17. To give an adequate English equivalent of the Greek *Parakletos* is notoriously difficult but there is much to be said for the use of the word Interpreter. The help which the Spirit is envisaged as giving is essentially help towards the true understanding of the mystery of Christ and His work. Through the guidance of the Spirit disciples will recognize that the Son is in the Father and they in the Son. They will call to mind what Christ has told them and understand it more deeply. The Spirit of truth will guide into all truth as He makes known the meaning of the things about to come to pass. It is significant that just as the meaning of a sentence or passage cannot be captured until the sequence of words is complete, so the work of the Spirit as Interpreter could not become effectual until Jesus had been glorified: that is to say until the sequence of His signs and words, His lifting up in death and resurrection, was complete. Only then could the Spirit show the meaning of these events in the light of God's all-embracing purpose. It was then that the risen Lord could breathe on His disciples and impart to them the Spirit that had guided Him in all His obedience to the will of His Father.

The seventeenth chapter of the Fourth Gospel, which records the intimate prayer offered by Jesus on the eve of His crucifixion, has for long been regarded as one of the highest peaks of the Christian revelation. Nowhere in the New Testament is the relation between God and Christ and the Church expressed in a more striking way. The Church is conceived, not so much in terms of its worship or its witness or its organization, but rather in terms of its growth in the knowledge of God and of His revelation. The Church consists primarily of Jesus' disciples to whom He, the supreme Teacher, has manifested the name of the true God. Beyond them, however, there stretches into the future an ever expanding number of those who come to believe on this same God through the disciples' testimony to the truth. The image is consistent with the whole emphasis of the Gospel. The only-begotten Son, the Word, Who has intimate knowledge of the Father, discloses this secret to a select band of those who are ready to listen to His teaching and to observe his works. They in turn, when instructed by the Spirit, go forth to perform a similar mission and others come to believe on God through their words and their works. The Church is, in its profoundest quality, the mystical company of all faithful people who know the true name of God and behold His glory in the person of the only-begotten Son.

But how is the Church constituted and how is its life maintained? Has the Church, when conceived in this way, no need for set forms or appropriate rituals? It would be, to say the least, paradoxical if the Gospel which lays so great stress on Jesus' use of symbolic acts and pictorial language should pay no attention to the sacraments which were undoubtedly being already used within the Church at large. And it is the judgment today of most commentators that the incidents recorded in the third and sixth chapters of the Gospel must contain allusions to the two dominical sacraments even if their pattern is not clearly defined. By the end of the first century A.D. the two sacraments were, as Professor W. F. Howard described them, "the two focal points in the Church's teaching". Jesus' own ministry had begun with 'water' and ended with 'blood'. Hence it is legitimate to assume that the author of the

Gospel considered the sacraments of 'water' and 'blood' to be essential elements in the discipleship of all who wished to dwell in the Truth. But it would be fatal if these sacraments came to be regarded as nothing more than ritual forms. Their place in the Church depended entirely upon the Spirit Who would take them and interpret them and use them as means to lead believers into the deepest mysteries of the faith.

The incident recorded in the third chapter is most revealing. Nicodemus, a man of learning, a leading interpreter of the Law which he regarded as God's supreme revelation to men, came to Jesus to discover what new light He might throw upon the sacred writings. He was presumably ready to receive new comments and even to make new adjustments. But Jesus' reply was quite radical. The altogether new has come. An altogether new perspective is required. The Law was given by Moses but grace and truth have come in the new revelation. To receive the new disclosure of truth nothing less than a birth from above is needed, the birth mediated in sacramental form through water and confirmed by the Spirit. Had not Jesus Himself inaugurated his new ministry of teaching the secrets of the Kingdom of God and of the Messiah by passing through the water? So must Nicodemus and all serious searchers for the Truth be ready to pass through the humble door of entrance if they would gain access to the vision of the invisible world of ultimate reality and learn its meaning.

Similarly in the sixth chapter of the Gospel it is to seekers after bread from heaven that the words about the bread of life are spoken. They will not find bread from heaven through a sudden miracle bringing a new kind of manna or a regular provision of daily food. The bread of God is that personal life which comes down from heaven and gives life to the world. But how does He mediate that life? Certainly through His words which are the expression of His own essential being. But not only through His words. Words can become actions and the life of the Son of Man is conveyed in sacrifice on the Cross. This is the fundamental disclosure. Yet it is most unlikely that the words interpreting this disclosure bear no relation to the sacrament of the Eucharist which at the time of the writing of the Gospel was well established in the Church. For Jesus at the heart of the discourse says:

> "Unless you eat the flesh of the Son of man and drink His blood you have no life in you; he who eats my flesh and drinks my blood has eternal life and I will raise him up at the last day. For my flesh is meat indeed and my blood is drink indeed. He who eats my flesh and drinks my blood abides in me and I in him" (John 6. 53-56).

Here is the *truth* of the Eucharistic meal, only to be received by those who allow the words of the Divine Word to be made meaningful in their own hearts and minds through the ministry of the Spirit. It is the Spirit alone who gives meaning and through meaning quickens to new life. But the Spirit uses words and actions and simple household necessities like water and bread and wine to convey, within the mystical life of the Church, the ultimate realities of the heavenly order to the hearts and minds of the faithful.

c. *The Life Everlasting*

It is characteristic of the seeker after truth and meaning
that he is not interested in events either of the past or of the
future *for their own sakes*. He is interested in them only as they
contribute something to his ultimate quest. If events of the
past point forward to a fulfilment and that fulfilment seems
either to have come to pass already or at least to be near,
then obviously there is meaning in the total complex,
promise and fulfilment included. If again it appears that
events in the future will substantiate and integrate movements now becoming visible, then in the same way some
meaning in the whole process can be inferred. Yet the
searcher for meaning can never rest content with partial
realizations. He feels compelled to strive towards that all-
embracing truth which is capable of gathering together into
a single pattern all that has happened and that will happen.
Such a pattern can, by its very nature, depend little upon
particularities of space or time. It must embrace all places
and all times. And although by the very conditions of his
own existence man can never attain a definition of meaning
which is totally independent of the space-time structure,
yet he tries again and again to discover a technique or a
formula which will allow him to ascend into the transcendent and to enjoy the timeless quality of the eternal.

The unhesitating witness of the New Testament is that
such freedom can be found only within the experience of a
personal relationship. Where one person truly dwells in
another, structures of space and time are in large measure
transcended. And this experience, which may come only

fleetingly and occasionally in this life, is a foretaste of that which may give meaning to the whole. Certainly the New Testament speaks of an 'eternal life' which is virtually independent of the passage of time. It speaks also of a communion with God which is virtually independent of the place where men worship. "The hour is coming when neither on this mountain nor in Jerusalem will you worship the Father: the hour is coming, and now is, when the true worshippers will worship the Father in spirit and truth" (John 4. 21, 23, R.S.V.). "He who hears my word and believes Him who sent me, has eternal life; he does not come into judgment, but has passed from death to life . . . the hour is coming, and now is, when the dead will hear the voice of the Son of God, and those who hear will live" (John 5. 24-5, R.S.V.). Here are two definitive statements, the one describing a relationship relatively independent of space, the other of time. Through the mediation of the Son of God men can enter now, anywhere, into the possession of timeless, spaceless life.

This life-in-relationship which is believed to be the meaning of all existence receives two classic definitions in the New Testament. In the Fourth Gospel, where it is frequently affirmed that the believer already possesses what is called 'eternal life', this life is defined as "knowing thee the only true God and Jesus Christ whom thou hast sent". But what does it mean to 'know' God? Knowledge of a deity has meant very different things in different religious systems and this definition therefore must depend upon its wider context of meaning in the Fourth Gospel. From this it is clear that 'knowledge' is used to describe the perfect relationship which exists eternally between the Father and the Son. The Father knows the Son and the Son knows the Father. We might almost say the Father knows the truth or the depth of meaning personified in the Son and vice versa. The emphasis is not quite the same as when this relationship is described in terms of love. 'Knowledge' involves mind, contemplation, vision, understanding, though not in any abstract or analytical or impersonal way. To know is to bring all the powers of mind and imagination to bear upon the other in order to penetrate to the depth of the truth which the other represents.

If this is in any way a valid interpretation of the knowledge which exists between the Father and the Son, it means that 'eternal life' for man consists in an ever deepening penetration into the meaning of the revelation of God in Jesus Christ and this penetration can only be made by the guidance of the Holy Spirit. It is the Spirit Who as Helper or Interpreter opens the mind to understand the truth of the personal Word of God. "From his fulness have we all received, grace upon grace." "No one has ever seen God: the only Son, Who is in the bosom of the Father, he has made him known" (John 1. 16. 18, R.S.V.). There is in all this an exercise of the intellect or the imagination or a concentration of the mind, however we may care to express it. A personal relationship cannot come to fruition simply through the exercise of affection or even sacrificial action. There is the interplay of knowing and being known, of learning and being tested, of receiving insights and making intellectual response. In this process time seems to stand still: the place of meeting is irrelevant. Mind is related to mind and in the relationship the meaning and truth of all existence is discovered. "This is life eternal: to know thee who alone art truly God, and Jesus Christ whom thou has sent" (John 17. 3, N.E.B).

The other classic definition of the New Testament is to be found in the writings of St. Paul. Eternal life is simply an existence *in Christ*. No phrase is more characteristic of St. Paul's understanding of the Christian revelation than these two simple words. In Christ all the fulness of God was pleased to dwell. In Christ the eternal purpose of God has been realized. In Christ the meaning of the whole creation is brought to a focus. And now, from the other side, if any man is in Christ there is a new creation. Old canons of interpretation are obsolete—all has become new. In Christ the travail of creation takes on a profound meaning. In Christ the suffering of the individual is recognized as full of significance for the wider community. In Christ the alienation of man from man is resolved within a creative reconciliation. In Christ death is overcome and life reigns supreme. Those who are in Christ have already died to self, to sin, to death itself. In Christ they have been raised to fulness of life, a life which is hid with Christ in God.

St. Paul employs such a wealth of imagery that it is not always the timelessness of eternal life that is emphasized. When surveying the vast sweep of human history and its dénouement at the end or when thinking of the Kingdom of God and its ultimate establishment over all hostile powers, he moves within the framework of a time-flow leading forward to glory and vindication at the end. But when he returns to his favourite phrase *in Christ*, space and time are transcended. To know Christ, to be found in Christ, to be crucified and risen with Christ, to enjoy all spiritual blessings in Christ—such expressions are virtually

157

independent of time-categories. Eternal life is here and now in Christ and its meaning is perceived ever more fully through the assistance of the Spirit who perfectly comprehends the thoughts and purposes of God. For what no eye has seen nor ear heard nor the heart of man conceived, what God has prepared (in a certain sense in the future) for those who love Him, God has (already) revealed to us through the Spirit.

Chapter Seven

I BELIEVE IN GOD

MY brief survey of what I regard as the four definitive patterns of Biblical imagery is now complete. In Chapter 2 I considered four major questions with which man, I believe, has been compelled to grapple at all times and in all places. I then tried to see whether the Christian faith, as presented in the Bible, speaks relevantly to these questions. In this enquiry I have looked neither for simple answers nor for neat solutions. The Bible deals all the time with living situations, its answers spring out of living human experiences. By examining the four inter-related patterns of imagery as they emerge in the Biblical literature it has been possible to see the great questions of human existence being answered through the revelation of the nature and activity of the living God in Christ.

Can we now summarize the results of this survey within a tentative credal form? From the very beginning of the Christian mission men have tried to encapsulate the essential Christian message in a form that could easily be remembered and to which reference could easily be made. Perhaps the simplest of all such forms, which must at a very early stage have established itself in the Church, is that which today we call The Grace and which we constantly use in our services of worship: "The grace of our Lord Jesus Christ and the love of God and the fellowship of the

Holy Spirit be with us all." The most recent attempt to frame a confession of essential Christian faith is that of the World Council of Churches which has now accepted as its basis: "The World Council of Churches is a fellowship of churches which confess the Lord Jesus Christ as God and Saviour according to the Scriptures and therefore seek to fulfil together their common calling to the glory of the one God, Father, Son and Holy Spirit." Always the problem has been how much to include and how much to omit. If too little is said there can easily be misunderstanding: if too much there can equally be confusion and lack of any clear definition.

I

The most famous of all attempts to define essential Christian doctrine are embodied in the creeds which we call the Apostles' and the Nicene. Each of these creeds may be regarded as representing certain widely accepted emphases in the early Church. The Apostles' Creed represents the numerous credal forms of Roman or Western Christianity, the Nicene those of Eastern Christianity. It appears that every leading Church in early times had its particular variant both of creed and liturgy but as possibilities of communication and co-ordination between the churches became more numerous in the fourth and succeeding centuries, the movement towards greater uniformity gathered momentum and two basic forms gained wide acceptance. I propose to glance at these two historic creeds before summarizing the results of my own enquiry.

The first clause is virtually the same in each creed. It confesses God as Father, Almighty, Creator. It would have been acceptable to the devout Jew though he might not have put Fatherhood in the forefront and might not have regarded the eastern addition of "things visible and invisible" as necessary. The clause is exceedingly brief and although its long use has established it firmly in the Church's faith it is still in order to ask whether it is comprehensive enough to represent the majestic witness of the Biblical revelation as a whole.

The third clause shows a marked difference between West and East. In the Apostles' Creed, the clause focuses attention solely upon the Holy Spirit in action—in the life of the Church, in the forgiveness of sins (with a probable reference to baptism) and in the gift of everlasting life. In the Nicene Creed, however, there is a notable series of relative clauses defining more precisely the essential nature of the Spirit—proceeding from the Father and the Son, worshipped and glorified with the Father and the Son, pre-existent and speaking through the prophets (of the Old Testament dispensation). It is questionable how far the clause, whether in West or East, is really satisfactory. Clearly in each case the confession was related to the particular situation which existed in the second, third and fourth centuries of the Church's life. At that time the Church was threatened by pneumatic sects such as the Montanists, the Divine status of the Spirit operating in the Church was under debate and the concern about resurrection to eternal life was paramount. But the confession of the nature of the Spirit's activities is too limited in its scope and includes too much that is derivative rather than primary. It must surely be judged an inadequate summary of the Biblical testimony to the nature and activity of the Spirit.

The second clause is quite the most substantial both in West and East. This is not surprising seeing that the altogether *new* thing to which Christians bore witness was that the Messiah had come into the world and that through the work which He had accomplished, salvation was now available to all believers. This was the burden of early Christian preaching—that Jesus of Nazareth, born of David's line, having been attested by the mighty works which God enabled Him to do, had been crucified and buried, and had then been raised up on the third day and exalted to the right hand of God. This Jesus was Messiah and Lord and salvation could be found only through His name.

As can readily be seen, it is this proclamation which occupies the largest space in the second clause though additions were made both in West and East. In the West the question of how the Messiah came into the world had to be answered in view of heretical assertions that He, a man, had been at a certain stage in His career raised to the status of the divine. The birth stories of the Gospels of Matthew and Luke were summarized in the affirmation that the Son of God was conceived by the Holy Ghost, born of the Virgin Mary. In the East the question had to be taken still farther back in view of assertions that He, though miraculously brought into the world, had yet been *created* in the aeons of the past and must be regarded as subordinate to the Creator God. Phrase after phrase is used to establish the image of the Christ as *begotten*, God out of God, of one substance with the Father. Then, as in the West, the entrance into human life is described as by the Holy Ghost of the Virgin Mary.

The conclusion to the second clause is virtually the same

in both creeds, each in its own way affirming that the exalted Messiah will come to judgment and thus establish His kingdom for ever. One slight variant has found a place in the Western creed—the reference to the descent into hell. This phrase does not appear in any creed before the middle of the fourth century and must be regarded as having won ultimate acceptance because of its bearing upon questions which were being asked from the very beginnings of Christian history about the welfare and destiny of those who had died before the coming of Christ and His Gospel. That Christ through His death descended to the abode of departed spirits is implied in the New Testament but it is questionable whether such a phrase should find a permanent place in a definitive Christian creed. As I have already suggested, the crucial difficulty in any attempt to summarize essential Christian doctrine is to know what to include and what to omit. In my judgment the second clause of the two official creeds of Christendom contains too much. Certain phrases could well have been left in their contexts in the New Testament, whence they could have been related, as need arose, to the particular vocabularies and patterns of imagination of particular periods of history. A summary can best fulfil its purpose by concentrating its attention upon the definitive affirmations which are related to the human situations at all times and in all places. Other matters can be dealt with in the light of Scripture and accumulated Christian experience as occasion arises.

I turn now to the four patterns of imagery which we have examined in their Biblical context and I propose the following summary:

I believe in
God

| Father | Redeemer | King | Creator |

through
Jesus Christ

| Son of God | Saviour of the World | Lord of glory | Word of life |

in
The Holy Spirit

| Of Love | Of Liberty | Of Discipline | Of Truth |

In this summary the threefold confession of God, beyond, with, and in us is set out vertically: the fourfold pattern of imagery is set out in three horizontal rows and the vertical correspondences can be readily observed. I claim no finality for the titles or abstract nouns which I have selected but generally speaking they are derived from the Bible and they express, I believe, the chief emphases which my survey has revealed. I shall now comment briefly on each element in the total pattern.

II

I BELIEVE IN GOD. The word 'God', it may be urged, is an extraordinarily slender peg on which to hang the weight of so comprehensive a faith. Yet some word must be used. It is indeed true that a single word from any language can all too easily become hackneyed, worn and commonplace. The awe and wonder which originally surrounded the name of the most holy can evaporate completely and the word can be degraded to the level of an expletive. Or the name can come to represent so limited and circumscribed a being that the plea begins to be made for the recognition of a hidden God or of a God above God. Or if the semanticist wishes to analyse the word and to discover its meaning by examining its antecedents, the believer may be tempted to exclaim that "God only knows what 'God' means".

The difficulties are immense. But how can we speak of Him Who is our ultimate concern, Him to Whom we owe an absolute allegiance, Him from Whom we receive un-bounded grace (that is if we are in the least aware of having such a concern or of recognizing such a relation) except by naming Him? To name Him lightly and super-ficially is to show at once that no true understanding exists and that the title is being used in vain. To name Him in a vacuum, with no relation to the one who speaks or to the world or to mankind at large is also futile. The word 'God' in isolation is meaningless. The believer who begins therefore by affirming his faith in God must necessarily go on to amplify his confession in terms which are best described as *appropriate* to the name to which they are related. To take a vivid illustration of Sidney Hook's, few would not shrink from speaking of God, either in discourse or in prayer, as 'Our Nephew in Heaven'. Such language is simply inappropriate. It finds no support in the religious history of mankind and makes no appeal to current religious experience. Our task therefore is to seek constantly for language which is *appropriate*, both in the sense of being true to the highest revelations of the past and of being relevant to the deepest needs of man-in-society today. The whole thesis of this book is that the writings of the Bible provide us with the most appropriate language that could be desired; always making allowance for such translations to establish themselves as are appropriate for our own day.

Father. Whatever the structure of the family may be in any particular period or in any cultural milieu, the name 'father' is given to him from whom the family derives its life and through whose providential care that life is sustained. Mystery may surround the processes by which this life is generated and maintained but that the father-figure is the fount and origin of the family's existence is one of the most widespread assumptions of mankind. Even today when the father's place in the family tends to become less important, when the very conditions of modern life cause him to be physically present in the home to a quite limited extent, and when his personal responsibility for the care and protection of the family may often seem minimal, the name father still retains an element of 'beyond-ness' in the vocabulary of the home which no other title carries. Certainly in Biblical times, as the remarkable prayer in Ephesians 3 so clearly shows, a family derived its very coherence from the father and this leads the author of the prayer to affirm that every family, wherever it may be, depends for its origin and its continuance upon the one Father who is the object of our worship, the Father of us all.

As we saw in an earlier chapter, this is the name which Jesus used in His most elevated teaching as well as in His most intimate prayers. All life is derived from the Father and by Him all life is sustained. Not a sparrow falls to the ground without the Father. It is not His will that a single little one should perish. He feeds the birds, He clothes the grass, He gives good gifts to all who ask. His all-embracing providence seeks to gather those to whom He has given life into a relation of conscious sonship. The very structure of the family is forgiveness—the Father forgiving the children's trespasses and the children forgiving one another. The name is the simplest of all Divine titles and yet perhaps the most far-reaching in its implications. Though so intimate and gracious it speaks also of transcendence for the father is always before the child and above the child. It holds an impressive place in one of the earliest credal forms.

> For although there may be so-called gods in heaven or on earth—as indeed there are many 'gods' and many 'lords'— yet for us there is one God, the Father, from whom are all things and for whom we exist (1 Cor. 8. 5-6, R.S.V.).

The Christian confession of God as Father is not likely to lose its appropriateness or its relevance unless the time ever arrives when home and family are swallowed up in a monochrome collective society.

Redeemer. It is not easy to select the most appropriate title from amongst those of the Old Testament which celebrate the dramatic acts by which God has saved and still saves His people. A verb usually translated 'deliver' is constantly employed in this connexion and the English noun Deliverer, though not a very happy word, might well be used to define this area of God's activity. Or there is the verb 'save', with the occasional reference to the Saviour of Israel. The advantage of the word 'redeem' is that it speaks so power-fully of freedom gained. It is the characteristic word used to describe the gracious act of God in breaking the bonds which held the Hebrews enslaved in Egypt and bringing them out into new possibilities of freedom. Though the root of the word contains a reference to buying a slave out from his bondage, this precise definition is soon transcended. To redeem is to release from every form of constriction, physical or moral, and to lead out into a new sphere of expansiveness and health. In ordinary usage today, redeem and redemptive are noble and challenging words. The title Redeemer is worthy to be used in describing what God has ever been ready to do on behalf of His people.

A further advantage in the word 'redeemer' is that it automatically carries a *personal* reference. When a man is in a position of great danger and then suddenly deliverance comes, the whole episode may pass with scarcely any personal contact between the victim and his deliverer. But in the case of redemption, the redeemer not only deals with the enslaving powers but also acts personally on behalf of those who are thus redeemed. He comes from 'beyond', the area of freedom; he exercises powers superior to those of the forces of tyranny. The very title 'Redeemer' therefore points to the transcendent. At the same time He, the Redeemer, takes upon himself the cost of the struggle for freedom and having won the victory leads the newly-emancipated out into newness of life. In the Old Testament the particular vocabulary of redemption is to be found in such Psalms as 103 and 107 and in Chapters 40-66 of the Book of Isaiah. There is the backward look to the great redemption from Egypt, there is the forward look to the redemption from Babylon. So assured is the latter that it can be regarded as already accomplished. "Fear not, O Israel, for I have redeemed thee. I have called thee by thy name: thou art mine." This is the pattern of God's redemption for all time. He redeems from every constricting form of bondage: He calls men out to a new form of service which is itself perfect freedom.

King. Again it is not easy to choose the most appropriate title for the central figure who integrates and co-ordinates the life of the city. Ruler, emperor, sovereign are possibilities but in spite of the tendency in this century to turn away from the institution of kingship, I still think that *King* is the best title of all. It has a wealth of Scriptural precedents behind it and it would be impossible to expunge it from our own culture without leaving serious gaps in our drama and literature. There have been bad kings in plenty and some of the worst examples of kingly cruelty and injustice were to be found in the world at the beginning of the Christian era. Nevertheless the Old Testament did not hesitate to give the title King to the Lord's Anointed and in its doxologies the New Testament gives praise to the King eternal, immortal, invisible, who reigns for ever and ever.

Kingship has normally been associated with elements of pomp and grandeur but those are only secondary accompaniments to the primary task of the king which is to establish justice and order for his people. He promulgates laws which regulate the total life of the community in relation to persons and property. He watches for injustice and seeks to remove it. He is particularly concerned for the cause of the needy and the oppressed. He willingly takes his place at the hub of the social order and acts as the centre of coherence in all disputed matters. Ideally he binds together earth and heaven in one harmonious whole. By his very nature, as the centre and the apex of the community, the king occupies a position of transcendence. He represents the majesty of the law. He is compelled to act in judgment when law has been infringed. So this title is apt as a symbol of transcendence even though few political societies today retain the institution of kingship under this precise name. So long as records remain of the part taken by kings in the ordering of human society, so long will it continue to be appropriate to worship God as King and to pray that His Kingdom may come.

Creator. No faith is complete which does not seek to come to terms with the universe to which man belongs, its meaning and its purpose. To say that it means nothing, that all is anarchy and chaos, is the mark of final despair. Few have committed themselves to such a judgment. The majority, even though unable to make any clear affirmation about what the universal process signifies, have clung to the belief that some kind of beneficent providence is in control of the world and that the end will not be sheer futility. To express this in words it has been customary to say that the world has been created. Even those who would be quite unwilling to posit a personal Creator yet speak freely of creation at a point in time or of continuous creation. It may, indeed, be asked whether creation is the appropriate term to use if no personal Creator is in view. Emergent evolution or spontaneous appearance would then seem to be more accurate descriptions of the way in which the universe has reached its present form.

Creation, I suggest, normally implies four things. First the existence of a personal creator. Second a design in the creator's mind. Third the existence of material ready to be fashioned to the design envisaged. Fourth the activity by which the plan is brought to fulfilment. In the world of art from which these language-forms are taken the artist first sees his vision and then proceeds to work it out, using whatever instruments may be appropriate, shaping and re-shaping stone, clay, sounds, paint or whatever the material may be. To extend this pattern to the universe as a whole and to give the title Creator to Him Who has envisaged the universal plan raises at once the difficulty that *ex hypothesi* there can be no antecedent material available for the Creator to use. Hence in traditional Christian theology it has been affirmed that the creation of the universe was *ex nihilo* (out of nothing), a statement which robs the original analogy of much of its force and appropriateness.

Unquestionably there are difficulties in using the tradi-tional name Creator for God and yet it is hard to suggest an alternative. It is possible to insist that the word 'create' as used in the Bible was an artistic rather than a scientific term and that its use by scientists has not served the interests of clarification. If however the precise scientific reference is omitted, it then becomes possible to imagine the universe as a meaningful whole and as the work of personal mind shaping available materials. Whence the materials came, the Bible does not enquire. That a formless concentration of energy might have existed with God before the creation of the world does not seem to me an impossible conception to entertain. Whether or not this is regarded as acceptable or whether we must fall back upon *creatio ex nihilo*, the all-important element of this confession of faith is its affirma-tion of God's transcendence—its assurance that the source and inspiration of the total created order is the personal Creator God. The 'how' of creation remains a mystery. That the universe whose marvellous structure has become increasingly known to us depends entirely upon the will of a personal Creator is an essential part of the Christian confession.

Through Jesus Christ. In another primitive credal form we find the striking affirmation:

> There is one God and
> There is one mediator between God and men,
>   the man Christ Jesus (1 Tim. 2. 5, R.S.V.).

'Through Jesus Christ' is an abridged form of this statement and it carries the implication that we both receive and express our faith in God *through Him*. The title Jesus Christ leads us immediately into the world of space and time for He was Jesus of Nazareth whose home was in Palestine and Who suffered and died outside the city of Jerusalem: at the same time he was the Christ, the heaven-sent Messiah, looked for by the Jews but acclaimed by Christians as risen from the dead and glorified. The very name Jesus Christ is an epitome of the Gospel. Jesus went about doing good and healing all who were oppressed of the devil, whom they slew and hanged on a tree: but God raised him up and made that same Jesus who was crucified both Lord and Christ. 'Through Jesus Christ' identifies the figure, human and divine, who is the focus of our concern. The titles which follow will symbolize the ways in which He is the mediator between God and man, bringing the majesty of the transcendent God within the compass of a human life, lifting up humanity to its true destiny within the compass of the life which is divine.

Son of God. The title 'Son' as normally used contains three main ideas. The first is that of physical generation—that the son is the offspring of the father: the second is that of likeness—that the son reveals as no one else can the character of the father: the third is that of relationship—that the son enjoys a unique access to the father's heart.

In regard to the physical generation of Jesus, the evidence of the New Testament lacks clear definition. St. Paul declares that the Son of God 'was descended from David according to the flesh' (Rom. 1. 3) and that He was 'born of woman' (Gal. 4. 4, R.S.V.). Neither the author of the Epistle to the Hebrews nor the author (or authors) of the Johannine writings make any reference to the physical birth. Both St. Matthew and St. Luke trace the physical genealogy of Jesus to its remote origins and each in his own way tells of the conception by the Holy Spirit and of birth through the womb of the Virgin Mary. It seems impossible on the basis of this evidence to construct any clear and unified witness concerning the physical descent and birth of Jesus. The tradition is strong that this child was not born as a result of the ordinary cohabitation of a human pair. God willed that His Son should enter into the world in a unique way and Mary was chosen to be the mother of the only-begotten Son of God. The exact physical processes we cannot know and do not need to know. The central affirmations concern the gracious initiative of God and the birth in the womb of a human mother of the Divine Son.[1]

Proceeding to moral likeness, we find ourselves on

[1] See J. Burnaby, *The Beliefs of Christendom*, pp. 84-87

altogether firmer ground. The New Testament writers all claim, in one way or another, that this Son was the perfect image of the Father. No man has seen God at any time but the only Son, who is in the bosom of the Father, has unveiled Him. He, says St. Paul, is the likeness of God. He reflects the glory of God and bears the very stamp of His nature, says the writer of the Epistle to the Hebrews. He that hath seen me hath seen the Father, Jesus is recorded to have said to Philip. The pattern of the Son's life on earth is the untarnished reflection of the Father's life in heaven.

The third idea naturally follows. The relationship of the Son with the Father is unique. This is one of the central themes of the Fourth Gospel but it is to be found in other parts of the New Testament. "All things have been delivered to me by my Father; and no one knows the Father except the Son and anyone to whom the Son chooses to reveal Him" (Matt. 11. 27, R.S.V.). No words could more clearly express the uniqueness of the relationship between Jesus, the Son of God, and His Father. Without reserve Jesus is acclaimed to be the Son of God Who reveals to man the nature of true sonship and opens the way for man to attain his own true status as a son of God.

Saviour of the World. In both Old and New Testaments, salvation is a dominant theme. And although the term Saviour is seldom applied to Jesus directly, no title expresses more succinctly the testimony of the earliest Christian witnesses. God whose nature and property it is to redeem His people out of all their afflictions, has sent His Messiah to enact the great comprehensive redemption of all the ages: He is indeed the Saviour of the world. And if one event beyond all others can be regarded as the vindication of His saving power, it is the resurrection from the dead. He, the Messiah, had been crucified but the pangs of death could not hold Him. Not even the universal processes of corruption could touch Him. God raised Him up and thereby designated Him the Saviour of all who would turn to Him and become partakers of His salvation.

This emphasis which is so strongly represented in the early preaching of the Apostles is expanded in an impressive fashion in the Gospel of St. Mark. This Gospel might justly be called the Salvation-Gospel. It shows how Jesus was initiated into His work as Saviour through the waters of baptism. It goes on to tell of His saving ministry to the sick, the paralysed, the demon-possessed, the diseased, and above all the sinful. It makes clear that those who desire to share in this ministry must themselves first share in His baptism and cup (sacramentally and in action). It leads on through the Passion and the Death to the great Victory, with the risen Christ leading His disciples to Galilee, partners in the new covenant of salvation. He, the Saviour, has identified Himself completely with the human lot: as the writer of the Epistle to the Hebrews was to say later, He, the pioneer of salvation, was made perfect through suffering: and now He is able to save to the uttermost all who draw near to God *through Him*.

In this whole context 'save' is a richly comprehensive word. It denotes not only deliverance from bondage of every kind—social tyranny, natural corruption, demonic possession, fear and guilt, sin and death—but also deliverance into freedom of every kind—physical, political, personal. Christians were convinced that the God Who had raised the Saviour's body from corruption and death would also raise up their mortal bodies. They were convinced that the God Who through Jesus had won the victory over all the powers of darkness and evil would save them out of the clutch of every kind of tyranny—earthly or demonic. Above all they were convinced that the dominion of sin had been broken by the saving act of Christ. There was little theorizing about temptation and the fall and corporate guilt and individual sin in the early Church. The facts of outward degradation and inward remorse were inescapable. Yet from all this the salvation wrought by the one Saviour had set men free. United with him through baptism into His death, covenanted with Him through sharing in the new testament in His blood, men became more than conquerors through Him Who had loved them and given Himself for them.

The Lord of Glory. This title, though rarely used in the New Testament, links together in a striking way the themes of Lordship and Glory which figure so prominently in the witness to the exaltation of the risen Messiah. Not only had God raised Him from the dead, breaking thereby every form of human enslavement. He had raised Him up and given Him glory, exalting Him to the right hand of His majesty and giving Him a name above every name; "let all the house of Israel know assuredly that God hath made that same Jesus whom ye have crucified both Lord and Christ" (Acts 2. 36). *Jesus is Lord* became the most notable confession of the early Church.

It is one of the most remarkable features of early Christianity that a title which had stood in the Greek version of the Old Testament for the Divine name, was transferred

176

to the ascended Jesus in Greek-speaking circles. How exactly this came about can only be conjectured. Probably the early Christians in Jerusalem used the Aramaic title *Mar* as they worshipped their leader who had been taken up into the heavenly places and this title in turn was translated into Greek as *Kyrios* (Lord). Whatever the stages in this process may have been, it is certain that the title which came rapidly to be adopted and which gathered into one the obedience and adoration of the early Church, was that which is translated into English as *Lord*. The title 'King' seems normally to have been avoided, perhaps because of the delicate political situation. But in naming Jesus 'Lord', men confessed Him as having been exalted to the highest place in the Divine economy, as sharing in the Kingship exercised by God Himself and as worthy to receive worship such as had formerly been reserved for the Eternal King. We may today employ current terminology and speak of the exalted Christ as God's viceroy, vicegerent, governor, to whom full authority has been delegated. But for the early Christians one title surpassed all others for it possessed Old Testament antecedents and carried implications which could hardly be missed in the Greek-speaking world. This was the title *Lord*. God Himself is the King eternal. The Lord of Glory exercises authority in His Name.

For those who acknowledged Christ Jesus as Lord two main consequences followed. Their worship and their ethical obedience must both be directed to God through Him. Henceforward His example and His teachings are the norms by which life in God's Kingdom must be measured. In St. Matthew's Gospel, which might be called the Gospel of the Kingdom, we find Jesus speaking with authority concerning those ethical standards and decisions which must characterize the life of its citizens. His own prayers and service are such as belong wholly to the Kingdom of God. In St. Paul's writings the implications of the Lordship of Jesus are drawn out again and again. At His name every knee must bow and every tongue confess that Jesus Christ is Lord. All varieties of service in the Church are to be directed to the one Lord. He is the head over all things for the church which is His body: He is the chief corner-stone of the temple, another image of the church. And in the world at large, whatever the task of any believer may be, it is to be done heartily, as serving the Lord and not men, knowing that from the Lord the inheritance will be received as final reward. For the ultimate destiny of those who serve the Lord Christ is to reign with Him in His glorious kingdom, the kingdom which at length He will deliver to God the Father and God will be all in all.

The Word of Life. This splendid phrase occurs twice in the New Testament (Phil. 2. 16; 1 John 1. 1). In St. Paul's letter to the Philippians it refers undoubtedly to the Gospel. In the first Epistle of St. John it may carry the same connotation but it may also refer to Him Whose own words were words of eternal life (John 6. 68), to Him Who is called the Word and in Whom was life (John 1. 1, 4). Whether or not the phrase is used by John as a title, no title could in fact more adequately express the function of Jesus Christ as the creative meaning of the whole universe. For the Greek term translated 'word' refers specifically to meaningful utterance and 'life' is associated with the creative activity of God as He initiates and sustains the universe. Through Jesus Christ

Who is the Word of Life, God gives form and meaning to the whole created order.

All attempts to explain this process in more detail tend to lean heavily upon the work of the creative artist as it is known to us in ordinary human life. The architect for example perceives his mental vision in rough outline, he strives to work it out in a detailed way on paper or through models, and only then does the labour with stones and bricks and wood actually begin. The literary artist sees a myth or a poem or a novel in general imaginative vision, he wrestles with words in the effort to project his vision into an ordered form and only then can readers lay hold of the story or the poem and seek to discover its meaning for their own lives. Whatever variations there may be in these illustrative analogies, one element is common to all. There must be the vision, the essential pattern of words or lines or sounds in the mind of the artist, before creative work can begin. Further, that vision must itself be living and dynamic, not rigidly fixed from the beginning but flexible in relation to the environment within which it must work itself out. A word of life, a living image—these are essential in the creative labours of the true artist.

And the Word of Life has now been revealed in definitive human form. While the meaning of the travail of the universe seems hard to perceive and harder to express, a word of life is heard, at first faintly, then growing in strength and ultimately spoken in full dramatic power. This word was with God at the beginning of creation. It will be the pattern of the completed process. The word having been made flesh, there exists in actual human form a touchstone by which the whole can be tested and interpreted.

Those who receive Him as the secret and meaning of existence no longer walk in darkness but have the light of life. Those who reject Him go out into the night where all is dark and the universe a tale with no clear form or meaning. The supreme revelation comes to those who do not fear to include suffering and death within the manifestation of the word of life. The image which includes nail-prints and a wounded side represents the total integration of human experience. This is the Word of Life which was with the Father and was made manifest to us. Receiving this, our joy is complete (1 John 1. 4).

IV

In the Holy Spirit. The earliest Christian preaching directed man's eyes to Jesus of Nazareth, crucified and risen, but it also spoke of a new operation of the Holy Spirit in human hearts. The promises relating to the Messiah had certainly been fulfilled but so too had the great promise of a new outpouring of the Spirit. This Spirit was not indeed altogether unheralded and unknown. The Holy Spirit, it was believed, had been present in the great ages of Israel's past —in the time of the first Temple, and in the time of the great prophets. But only in the age of the Messiah would the Spirit be experienced in His fulness. This, the Apostles dared to proclaim, had in fact happened. They therefore called men to turn to God and to be baptized into the name of Jesus Christ. So could they be assured of the gift of the Spirit and of an intimate participation in the glories of the Messianic age. Henceforward men would know God through Jesus Christ in the power of the Holy Spirit.

The Spirit of Love. At the very beginning of the Old Testament we encounter a mysterious reference to the Spirit of God moving upon or brooding over the face of the waters. A few verses later we find a reference to the breath or spirit of God entering into man and making him a living soul. In other words the Spirit of God is the source and giver of all *life*. Yet even at this early stage life is not an end in itself. Life is in order to relationship. Life flows forth from God to His universe in order that it may flow back as love from the creatures that He has made. The Spirit is truly the Spirit of life but still more is He the Spirit of Love.

And at last there appeared upon earth One in Whom life was fully identified with love. "The living Father sent me and I live by the Father" (John 6. 57). "The Father loves the Son and has entrusted Him with all authority" (John 3. 35, N.E.B.). "That the world may know that I love the Father" (John 14. 31). Life and love are identified in the eternal relationship which exists between the Father and the Son. Or to express this truth in another way, the Spirit Who unites the Father and the Son in perfect relationship is the Spirit of a life of unbroken love. Wherever the Spirit is creating fresh life it is with the object that this life may become life-in-love, and it is the joyful witness of the New Testament that this object has been achieved in an altogether new way through the advent of the Son of God amongst men and above all through His own outpouring of love into the midst of human relationships: "I made known to them thy name, that the love with which thou hast loved me may be in them, and I in them" (John 17. 26, R.S.V.).

What this meant within the life of the community is

described in lyrical fashion by St. Paul in his letter to the Romans: "God's love has been poured into our hearts through the Holy Spirit which has been given to us" (Romans 5. 5, R.S.V.). New life had certainly come but it was life fulfilling itself in love, love which brought believers into relationship with the Son and through the Son to the Father. To be sure, the cold of selfishness and lovelessness in the world at large showed little sign of thawing. But a fire had been kindled which could not be quenched—the Spirit radiating warmth of compassion and affection (Phil. 2. 1). A seed had been planted whose growth was assured—and the fruit of the Spirit is love (Gal. 5. 22). It is the Spirit Who makes the love of Christ a living reality in human hearts and in turn catches up the smallest response of human love and conveys it to the Father through the Son. "Strengthened with might by His Spirit in the inner man, that Christ may dwell in your hearts by faith, that ye, being rooted and grounded in love, may know the love of Christ and be filled with all the fulness of God" (Eph. 3. 16-19).

The Spirit of Liberty. To a puzzled and dispirited band of disciples the promise was given: "You shall receive power when the Holy Spirit has come upon you", and for a period the access of *power* was the most characteristic mark of the Spirit's activity. This is not surprising when it is remembered that the early disciples were threatened by seemingly over-whelming odds. Political tyranny, ecclesiastical conservatism, the threat of torture and death, the forces of unseen evil—all were ranged against them. To break through into freedom they needed a power far beyond their own resources and if power is defined as "the possibility of self-

affirmation in spite of internal and external negation"
(Paul Tillich), then the Holy Spirit is rightly related to
Power. The power manifested in Jesus the Saviour, enabling
Him to overcome the forces of disease, degradation and
death which were despoiling God's world, was transmitted
to those who accepted His salvation, enabling them in turn
to manifest the same Spirit of power as they escaped from
their particular bondage and rejoiced in their new found
liberty.

This power has no kind of connection with the force
which crushes and terrifies. There is a revealing saying
recorded by some ancient authorities in the text of the 9th
Chapter of St. Luke. When certain villages of Samaria
refused to receive Jesus and in consequence two of His
disciples wished to call down a consuming fire from heaven
upon them, He replied: "You do not know what manner
of spirit you are of; for the Son of man came not to destroy
men's lives but to save them" (Luke 9. 55). The power of
the Spirit is, in fact, unto *salvation*, unto the liberation of
the whole person and the whole community. This is the
power of the resurrection for "if the Spirit of Him Who
raised Jesus from the dead dwells in you, he who raised
Christ Jesus will give life to your mortal bodies also
through His Spirit which dwells in you" (Romans 8. 11,
R.S.V.). It is the power of emancipation from sin for "the
law of the Spirit of life in Christ Jesus has set me free from
the law of sin" (Romans 8. 2, R.S.V.). An oft-quoted
saying affirms that all power tends to corrupt and if power is
directed towards domination the dictum is undoubtedly
true. But if power is directed towards salvation into true
liberty then this power is of God. It flows from the Father

to the Son and through the Son to the heirs of salvation. All is in the Holy Spirit Who transforms the possibility of self-affirmation into the power of salvation and thereby manifests in space and time the spectacle of former slaves being set free from guilt and fear and endued with courage and confidence to follow their Saviour out into the glorious liberty of the redeemed people of God.

The Spirit of Discipline. We have already encountered the paradox that freedom cannot flourish except within a framework of order. It is the same Spirit Who set men free by empowering them with the might of God who now works in their midst to establish an order agreeable to the rule of God. A relatively late writing of the New Testament expresses this aspect of the Spirit's activity quite tersely: God did not give us a spirit of timidity but a spirit of power and love and *discipline* (2 Tim. 1. 7). Discipline is an essential ingredient in the life of a community. Without it anarchy and confusion must ensue. So St. Paul writes to the Church of Corinth: "God is not a God of confusion but of peace" (1 Cor. 14. 33, R.S.V.)—peace denoting a total harmony in which proportion is preserved and power is ever balanced with power for the common good.

It may at first sight seem surprising that the New Testament lays so great stress upon the *obedience* of the Son of Man. It is easy today to associate obedience with servility but this is in no way implied in the New Testament emphasis. To do the will of God was to the Son sheer joy. To show by His unswerving obedience how good was the ordered discipline of the Kingdom of God was to God's vicegerent a supreme delight. To manifest to His disciples the discipline of God's new order was to communicate to them the nature

184

of the Spirit of harmony and righteousness and ultimate peace.

It is noteworthy that the nature of the Spirit of order is vividly revealed in the Epistles through the body and temple analogies as they are applied to the life of the Church. Where these are used, the reference to the Holy Spirit is unmistakable. It is the Spirit Who animates the Body: it is the Spirit Who dwells in the Temple. But as was already clear then and is still clearer today the human body is an exquisite example of orderly interdependence of an organic kind: the temple is an outstanding example of orderly interdependence of an artistic kind. The writer of the Book of Wisdom had affirmed that the Spirit of the Lord fills the universe and holds all things together (1. 7). Now St. Paul can affirm that in the realm of the personal and social, the Spirit fills the Divine community and holds it together in balance, in mutual forbearance and self-discipline, in ordered growth and co-operation, in a unity of direction towards the transcendent goal. Good order, it has been said, is the foundation of all that is good. It is the Spirit who creates and renews order, both in the realm of nature and the realm of grace. God looked upon His created order and saw that it was good. In the redeemed order the whole body, the whole building, will when complete be so bonded together that it will be a worthy dwelling-place for God in the Spirit.

The Spirit of Truth. The Word of Life has been manifested in the flesh of a man, in the events of a human career. It is unthinkable that this New Testament witness could be the imaginative fabrication of a few deluded men. Its constant appeal is rather to what men have actually seen and heard and handled. Their witness is to one who lived and taught and healed and suffered and died and rose again. They stake their very existence on the truth of that which they affirm. The definitive *Logos* or word of meaning has been spoken into the very midst of the process of human history. Here is the heart of the Christian Gospel.

But how is the meaning to be grasped by successive generations of humanity? How is the meaning of any natural structure or historical complex grasped? In brief the answer is through *symbols*. The scientist or the artist expresses in symbolic form his understanding of the world as he perceives it and others who share his common humanity are gradually led to share his vision and his understanding. Or again a community expresses its understanding of its own historic existence through symbolic media — usually words and actions — and others are incorporated into the same interpretation through sharing in the common symbolism. The world of symbols serves to promote coherence and meaning and to assist man in his never-ending search for truth.

The witness of the early disciples was given in word and in action. They believed that the Spirit gave them utterance to express through their words (and words are symbols) the significance of what God had done for men through the sending of His Christ. Further they believed that whenever they came together for the prayers and the breaking of the bread (and those were symbolic actions) the meaning of their common life was revealed through the operation of the same Holy Spirit. It was not until a later period in Christian history that artists, under the direction of the same Spirit, expressed through symbolic forms the meaning

186

of the created order as they saw it focused in Christ. Perhaps we have not yet reached the stage when scientists are prepared to any marked degree to discover the coherence of the universe as they perceive it in terms of a central Divine-human organism, living, dying and rising again.

Man's highest and most constructive characteristic is his symbol-forming capacity. Amidst the myriad symbols that he has constructed a few stand out as supreme concentrations of ultimate meaning: the Four Gospels, the Pauline Epistles, the historic creeds, the Gospel Sacraments. These are supreme gifts of God the Holy Spirit, taking the things of Christ and interpreting them through the words and actions of individuals and communities. But the work of interpretation goes on unceasingly as the same Spirit inspires a man here to express the meaning of the Word of Life through his painting, a man there to express it through his music: a community here to express it through the construction of a nobly integrated house of God, a community there to express it through the outpouring of service to suffering humanity. In all these ways the Spirit inspires understanding in those who create and give, leads to the awakening of understanding in those who receive and learn. In one sense Truth is once and for all. He, the Word of Life, is the Truth: the Truth has been for ever revealed in Him. Yet in another sense Truth is growing in depth, expanding in range, as the Word of Life is related to man's ever extending experience of the universe and knowledge of his part. The Truth is central: the Truth is universal. And the Spirit everywhere and always is applying the central to the universal, the moment of time to the total flow of human history from beginning to end.

Such a range of interpreting activity extends far beyond the limits of the human imagination. We take our place with the disciples in the Upper Room on the eve of the events which were to form the crisis of the ages and we wonder with them how we can know, how we can understand. To us as to them the promise still comes: I will not leave you without assistance: the Holy Spirit whom the Father will send in my name, will teach you everything: He will be with you for ever: He will guide you into all the truth (John 14. 18, 26, 16; 16. 13).